personnel practices

for
small
colleges

by ronald a. bouchard

**national association of college and university
business officers, in conjunction with the
college and university personnel association**

Library of Congress Cataloging in Publication Data
Bouchard, Ronald A.
    Personnel practices for small colleges.

    1. Small colleges—United States—Personnel management.   I. National Association
of College and University Business Officers.   II. Title.
LB2328.3.B68   378'.11   80-11868
ISBN 0-915164-08-6

Printed in the United States of America

Edited and Designed
By Lanora Welzenbach

contents

exhibits

foreword

This book was written to address the needs of (1) business officers who are responsible for the personnel function in small colleges, (2) directors of personnel in small institutions, and (3) members of personnel departments in larger institutions. The book underwent a comprehensive review and consensus process, resulting in a publication that the National Association of College and University Business Officers (NACUBO) and the College and University Personnel Association (CUPA) are pleased to offer as representative of good personnel practice. The Small Colleges Committee of NACUBO set forth the objectives for the project, with CUPA providing professional expertise—a joint effort to put basic information on personnel practices within easy reach of anyone responsible for this operation.

The idea for such a publication had its genesis in work for a manual on planning, budgeting, and reporting that was prepared under the auspices of a grant from The Ford Foundation in 1968. As a result of that effort, members of NACUBO's Small Colleges and Personnel Committees determined that there was a need for a guide to personnel administration in small institutions.

Leaders of CUPA expressed interest in cooperating in this work and in 1978 a Steering Committee was appointed to be responsible for overseeing the book. The Steering Committee was composed of members of the NACUBO Small Colleges and Personnel Committees and of CUPA representatives. The manuscript was circulated for review among more than 40 business and personnel officers, including members of the CUPA Research and Publications Advisory Committee.

Ronald A. Bouchard, who prepared the original manuscript, served as administrative assistant to the president for personnel services at Ball State University and later as director of personnel and employee relations at California State University-Northridge before becoming assistant vice president for personnel administration at the University of Virginia. Bouchard, who also contributed extensively to NACUBO's *Federal Regulations and the Employment Practices of Colleges and Universities,* is president of CUPA for 1980–81. Leonard D. Harper, director of personnel at the University of Oklahoma, worked with Bouchard on

Chapter 2, "Compensation," which replaces *Wage and Salary Administration for Smaller Institutions of Higher Education,* published by NACUBO in 1974.

The sample forms in the exhibits used to illustrate this book were contributed by a number of colleges and universities and CUPA gave permission for reprinting ten articles from its "How-to" series. The Steering Committee is grateful for this generous assistance in compiling material for the exhibits.

Staff members associated with the project were Frank Mensel, former executive director of CUPA; David Roots, public affairs associate, CUPA; M. J. Williams, director of special programs, NACUBO; and Lanora Welzenbach, staff associate for information and publications, NACUBO.

DEAN H. KELSEY
Chairman, Steering Committee

Steering Committee

Dean H. Kelsey, *Chairman*
Vice President for Business,
  Emeritus
Albright College

Alice C. Baker
Personnel Officer
Frances Marion College

Glen E. Brolander
Vice President for Financial
  Affairs
Augustana College

Leonard D. Harper
Director of Personnel
University of Oklahoma

Alan Heyneman
Associate Treasurer-Administration
The University of Rochester

Eugene Johnson
Comptroller
Hampton Institute

Marwin Wrolstad
Vice President for Business Affairs
  and Treasurer
Lawrence University

preface

The need for a practical guide to personnel administration in higher education—one that would provide fundamental materials for developing and maintaining a sound personnel program—has frequently been expressed by administrators in higher education, especially by those in small colleges, where both staff and expertise for the personnel function may be limited. The need for such a manual has become intensified because the 1960s and 1970s brought to the campus growing numbers of government regulations, which have direct impact on the personnel practices of all institutions.

Personnel Practices for Small Colleges has been written expressly to address this need. It is intended to be a "hands-on, how-to-do-it" guide, describing practical applications of personnel policies. It is not a book on theory, nor does it cover in detail all aspects of the personnel function. The book deals with staff employees and includes only indirect reference to faculty or to student employees.

Sample forms, contributed by a number of colleges and universities, are included; these may be adapted for use by any institution, regardless of size. The forms are intended as samples *only*; their use will necessarily vary from one college to another. Further, while the forms were chosen with care, it is not possible to insure that they comply in all respects with the many federal and state laws and regulations that affect employment practices and the privacy of information. Institutions should carefully review their personnel forms for such compliance.

It is virtually impossible to write about personnel management in higher education without including extensive reference to various laws and regulations. However, such references in this book have been kept to a minimum. In addition to these sources, the reader is referred to other publications that provide detailed analyses of government regulations and their implications; a primary source for this is *Federal Regulations and the Employment Practices of Colleges and Universities,* published by NACUBO. For general reference on personnel topics, a brief bibliography is provided on page 179.

1. employment

Modern, centralized personnel programs are rooted in a period immediately following the industrial revolution when industry recognized the advantages of centralizing its workforce procurement responsibilities. Thus, from the employment function grew the entire field of personnel management, which presently includes wage and salary administration, benefits administration, training and development, organizational planning, labor relations, safety, and others.

In general, colleges and universities did not begin to centralize campus employment for staff personnel until the mid-1940s, which was a rapid growth era in higher education because of the numbers of World War II veterans attending college with government assistance. Since then, centralization has proved to be an efficient organizational strategy for the procurement of employees.

In small colleges that do not have a personnel director, the responsibility for the personnel function is typically assigned to the chief business officer. This places related functions such as payroll, benefits, position budgeting, and personnel under one manager.

A successful personnel program is one in which all personnel activities are related; each is integral to the whole. Position descriptions are an example, as they may be used for recruiting employees, for assignment and training, for performance appraisal, for compensation decisions, and if necessary, as criteria for administration of disciplinary action in the case of poor performance.

Government Regulations

The comprehensive term "employment," as used in this book, includes practices for recruiting, selecting, assigning, retaining, and separating employees. Each of these activities has been seriously affected by laws and regulations designed to eliminate discrimination on the basis of race, religion, color, sex, age, national origin, or mental or physical handicap. In addition to federal laws and regulations, many states, counties, and municipalities have enacted similar legislation.

Following are some laws and executive orders that require change in traditional personnel practices.

Title VII of The Civil Rights Act of 1964, as Amended

This is the primary federal law with respect to discrimination in employment. It specifically prohibits such discrimination on the basis of race, color, religion, sex, or national origin. Furthermore, the law bars any practice which (1) results in a failure or refusal to hire any individual because of such person's race, color, religion, sex, or national origin; (2) results in discharge of any individual because of such person's race, color, religion, sex, or national origin; (3) differentiates between individuals with respect to compensation, terms, conditions, or privileges of employment because of such person's race, color, religion, sex, or national origin; and (4) limits, segregates, or classifies employees or applicants for employment in any way which would deprive or tend to deprive any individual of employment opportunities or otherwise adversely affect such person's employment status because of such person's race, color, religion, sex, or national origin.

The Pregnancy Discrimination Act, which became effective October 31, 1978, amends Title VII of the Civil Rights Act and makes illegal any employment policy or practice that denies equal employment opportunity to applicants or employees because of pregnancy, childbirth, or related medical conditions. It also requires disabilities caused by pregnancy, childbirth, or related medical conditions to be treated in the same manner as are other disabilities under any health or disability insurance or sick leave program.

Title IX of the Education Amendments of 1972, as Amended

This requires that no person in the United States shall, on the basis of sex, be excluded from participation in, be denied the benefits of, or be subjected to discrimination under any education program or activity receiving any federal financial assistance. The regulations require each institution to conduct a self-evaluation of its policies and practices in this regard.

Disputes have arisen concerning the applicability of these regulations to employment matters. The first, sixth, and eighth Circuit Courts of Appeals have ruled that Title IX regulations do not cover employment. The Supreme Court has denied review of appeals of these decisions; thus those decisions remain law for these three circuits.

Equal Pay Act

This was enacted in 1963 as an amendment to the Fair Labor Standards Act. It requires equal pay for males and females who perform equal work on jobs that require equal skill, effort, and responsibility, and are performed under similar working conditions. The 1976 U.S. Supreme Court decision in the case of *National League of Cities* v. *Usery* did not exempt colleges and universities from the provisions of this act.[1]

Executive Orders 11246 and 11375

These require federal contractors to take affirmative action in employment with respect to minorities and females. Affirmative action under these executive orders requires results-oriented steps to eliminate barriers for protected classes through the use of preestablished goals. Small colleges may or may not be federal contractors, but they can hardly escape the social pressures for adopting affirmative action as a part of institutional policy.

Federal Contractors

This refers to an institution with a federal contract (not grant) of $10,000 or more, and requires institutions to adhere to Executive Orders 11246 and 11375, but it does not require a written affirmative action plan unless the federal contract is for $50,000 or more and the institution has 50 or more employees. Although written affirmative action plans are not required for federal contracts of less than $50,000, the Department of Labor and the Equal Employment Opportunity Commission (EEOC) recommend written programs. Some states also require that specified employers maintain written affirmative action plans.

Age Discrimination In Employment Act of 1967, as Amended

This makes it unlawful for an employer to fail or refuse to hire, or to discharge, or to differentiate among individuals with respect to their compensation, terms, conditions, or privileges of employment because of age. The protected age range, initially 40 to 65, was expanded to age 70 by the 1978 amendments. These amendments include a specific provision that limits the protection of this law for faculty with tenure to age 65 until 1982.

The Rehabilitation Act of 1973, Sections 503 and 504

Section 503 of the Rehabilitation Act requires federal contractors to take affirmative action to employ and advance in employment qualified,

---

[1] National League of Cities v. Usery, 426 U.S. 833 (1976).

handicapped individuals. Section 504 requires that no otherwise qualified handicapped individual be solely by reason of handicap excluded
from participation in, be denied the benefits of, or be subjected to
discrimination under any program or activity receiving federal financial
assistance. Section 504 also includes a requirement for self-examination
and modification of possible discriminatory policies and procedures in
education programs and activities.

Each of the laws and regulations described above is explained in detail
in NACUBO's *Federal Regulations and the Employment Practices of Colleges and Universities.*

Employee Recruitment and Selection

Employee recruitment involves a variety of tasks and skills, including
personnel requisitions, the preparation of position descriptions, the consideration of recruiting sources, and preemployment screening, interviewing, and reference checks. The first consideration in the recruitment
of new employees is the establishment of a position control system.

Position Control System

Efficient management and utilization of human resources is essential
for any organization, but especially for colleges and universities, which
are labor-intensive, committing up to 70% or 80% of their operating
budgets for human resources. Most colleges utilize a "position
budgeting" concept for identification and control of personnel. This
identification system lends itself to a logical "position control" system,
which can be maintained manually on a visible index system or on a
computer.

If an institutional budgetary position control system does not exist, it
would be beneficial to develop one for the personnel operation. To create
a visible index file, a separate card with a separate position control number is used for each position. The position title or classification and the
incumbent employee's name are the basic information required. As a
position is vacated and subsequently refilled, that information is recorded, thus providing an employment history of the position. The use
of color-coded cards or labels provides an efficient method through
which full-time, part-time, and temporary positions can be identified.

The pay level of the job and any changes can be recorded, providing a
classification history of the position. Other pertinent information can
also be included, such as starting and termination dates of employees in
the job. The position control system can serve as an excellent source for
the development of statistical information. (See Exhibits $1A_1$ and $1A_2$.)

Employee control forms may also be used. These provide pertinent information about a given employee that is easily accessible to the personnel office. Such a form is typically a continuous historical record, even if an employee changes positions. (See Exhibit 1B.)

The position control system is equally valuable for identifying and maintaining a record of positions, whether the employment function is centralized or decentralized. However, it is recommended that employment be centralized and coordinated through one office. Duplication of effort and expense can be minimized through centralization and a valuable service can be provided to the entire campus community. Centralization of the employment function assists the college in controlling its unemployment compensation costs and insures coordination of "new hires" with employees "laid off."

Personnel Requisition

Centralization requires organization to be effective. A basic component of such organization is a "personnel requisition" or "employment requisition," a form that serves as the basis of an orderly procedure whereby departments and offices can notify the employment office of the need to fill a vacant position. Even if a college has limited personnel turnover, the use of such a form may prove advantageous because it produces a detailed history of each position. (See Exhibits $1C_1$ and $1C_2$.)

The personnel or employment requisition is recommended for initiating employment activity, since it indicates to the office responsible for employment such information as title of job, name of interviewing supervisor, date job is to be filled, special job requirements or qualifications, and whether the job is to be filled on a continuing, part-time, or temporary basis. If a college lacks position descriptions, a personnel requisition can easily be modified to incorporate basic job duties and responsibilities for recruiting and placement purposes.

Position Description and Job Specifications

When discussing personnel, the terms "job description," "position description," "job classification," and "job specifications" are frequently used interchangeably. They all refer to the same general activity of describing a job's duties, responsibilities, and qualifications, but technically each of the four have different nuances which distinguish one from the other. The reader may refer to the "Glossary" on page 176 for individual definitions of these terms. For the purposes of this book, discussion will be limited to the position description and job specifications.

A *position description* describes the duties required in a job or position and sometimes the qualifications or specifications required to perform the job. The latter, or *job specifications*, are typically expressed as minimum acceptable qualifications, such as education and experience, and sometimes as additional desirable qualifications. A position description, including the minimum qualifications, should be used as a basic reference document for recruiting and screening prospective staff members. This is essential to the employment process. (A detailed explanation of position descriptions is presented in Chapter 2.)

Job Relatedness Test: Griggs Decision

In 1971 the U.S. Supreme Court handed down the "Griggs decision" in the *Griggs* v. *Duke Power Company* case.[2] The case was filed under Title VII of the Civil Rights Act of 1964; out of this decision evolved the so-called "job relatedness" test. In essence, the Court stated that an employer might be unlawfully discriminating against applicants if it establishes, as a condition of employment, any job requirement that cannot be shown to be significantly related to successful job performance. For example, the requirement of high school graduation for a custodial position would probably fail to meet the job relatedness test.

The job relatedness criteria have significantly altered the traditional listing of minimum qualifications for jobs, specifically through the elimination of unnecessary qualifications. For example, experience qualifications are usually expressed as requiring fewer years of experience and educational requirements tend to be more pertinent.

Those responsible for establishing minimum qualifications should scrutinize them carefully against the Griggs criteria. Many supervisors are likely to list *maximum* rather than *minimum* job qualifications; therefore, those responsible for ultimate personnel decisions must carefully evaluate recommended qualifications to insure compliance with the job relatedness criteria.

Adverse Impact

In 1978 four federal agencies, the Equal Employment Opportunity Commission, Department of Justice, Department of Labor, and Civil Service Commission adopted the *Uniform Guidelines on Employee Selection Procedures*, thus unifying formerly diverse federal positions. College administrators should become familiar with these stringent guidelines because they embody the criteria that the regulatory agencies will use to measure "adverse impact."

---

[2]Griggs v. Duke Power Company, 401 U.S. 424 (1971).

Adverse impact occurs when there is a substantially different rate of selection in hiring, promotion, or other employment decisions which works to the disadvantage of members of a race, sex, or ethnic group. The guidelines offer a rule of thumb for determining such adverse impact. The rule states that adverse impact is present when the selection rate for any race, sex, or ethnic group is less than four-fifths or 80% of the selection rate for the group with the highest selection rate. (Groups constituting less than 2% of the available work force need not be included in this measurement.)

To illustrate, an adverse impact determination for a particular job (or group of jobs if the duties are similar) would begin with a finding of the selection rate for the job(s) being considered. If 100 Whites other than Hispanics apply for a job and 60 are hired, the selection rate would be 60/100 or 60%. To continue with this example, if the hiring rate for Blacks if 50% and for Hispanics, 20%—Whites having the highest rate at 60%—the impact ratio is computed as follows: Blacks 50/60 or 83%; Hispanics 20/60 or 33%. In applying the four-fifths or 80% rule, adverse impact is indicated for Hispanics since their selection rate is less than 80% (of the Whites).

Technically, adverse impact could be measured on a job-for-job, or decision-by-decision, basis. However, it is more likely that the regulatory agencies will be concerned primarily with the "bottom line" for all employment decisions. (The formula would otherwise be hardly meaningful for small numbers of decisions by smaller employers.)

If adverse impact is found, an employer must eliminate or modify the selection procedures which caused the adverse impact. If an employer decides not to do this, it must justify the use of the procedure on grounds of business necessity. This means that the employer must show a clear relation between the selection procedure and performance on the job. In effect, the employer must validate the procedure.

The impact of these guidelines is difficult to assess; actual case experience with federal agencies in the application and interpretation of the published guidelines and regulations is very limited at the time of this writing. However, the guidelines will probably result in significant changes in commonly accepted selection practices and procedures.

Recruiting Sources

A number of recruiting sources are available to colleges, including those described below.

Internal Candidates. Current employees of the college are an excellent recruiting source for job vacancies that occur above entry level. "Promotion from within" has several advantages: (1) it enhances employee morale by providing the opportunity for assuming jobs of greater responsibilities with increased remuneration; (2) it establishes career opportunities and encourages employees to remain with the institution, while offering managers a pool of applicants who are familiar with the institution's policies and procedures; and (3) it provides applicants whom managers have had the opportunity to observe firsthand with respect to performance capabilities and potential. The "job posting" process (see page 18), in which all job vacancies in the college are posted as they occur, affords interested employees the opportunity to apply.

Walk-in Applicants. The traditional, "walk-in" applicant pool is an inexpensive source of prospective employees. However, a college that receives a high number of walk-in applicants must analyze this pool to be sure it contains an acceptable balance of protected-class individuals. If protected classes are underrepresented in the pool—that is, if it lacks sufficient numbers of minorities and females as compared to the availability of these groups in the appropriate recruiting market—efforts must be made to develop a more representative applicant pool. Outreach programs may be required in which the college undertakes affirmative recruitment to attract minorities and females.

Referrals From Faculty and Staff. The referral of prospective employees by members of faculty or staff can be a good source of applicants. This source is often productive because a satisfied employee typically makes positive comments concerning the college to relatives, neighbors, and friends.

Generally, a current employee will refer only a well-qualified person, since a poor referral could reflect negatively on the employee. Lack of such referrals may indicate a dissatisfied work force or previous actions by the employer that have discouraged referral. A direct appeal or suggestion to faculty and staff will usually increase the applicant flow from this source. As with walk-in applicants, care must be taken to insure appropriate representation of the protected classes.

High Schools and Other Schools. Many technical, clerical, and secretarial support positions require no experience or limited experience; consequently, local high schools are often sources of prospective employees. Most business teachers and counselors will gladly share employment information with students. A college can make itself known to high school students through participation in job fairs and through volunteer activities such as explaining to students how to apply for a job or prepare for an interview. College participation in work-study programs, such as office internship programs, also generates applicants. If some students are exposed to the campus and find it a good place to work, they will carry the word back to others.

U.S. and State Employment Services. These employment services, which are operated on a unified basis in many states, are a potential recruitment source. However, colleges must be explicit about their job requirements or they may be confronted with many prospective employees who lack necessary qualifications and skills.

A representative of the college employment function should meet with an employment service representative and explain the procedure that the college desires to follow. The college should develop this contact so that one employment service representative can become familiar with the institution's needs. It may be necessary to ask that referrals be limited to specific job requests filed by the college. If these methods are used, an employment service can be an excellent source of applicants without cost to the college, since the services do not charge a placement fee.

Private Employment Agencies. These are another potential applicant source. Currently, it is common for an employer to assume the placement fee. With some agencies, the employer may decline payment of this fee and transfer it to the applicant, but this approach may restrict the number of referrals. If an institution's policy is *not* to pay placement fees, this should be indicated to the agency and to all persons who are referred. The level of service received from private employment agencies can be enhanced by working with one representative of the agency, who can become familiar with the operations and needs of the college.

Higher Education Administration Referral Service (HEARS). The Higher Education Administration Referral Service (HEARS) at One Dupont Circle, Washington, D.C. 20036, is an excellent source of administrative applicants for colleges. The HEARS service is currently sponsored by 19 higher education associations and actively recruits female and minority candidates.

Other Employers. To recruit candidates for higher-level professional and administrative positions, one may approach selected persons who occupy the same position at other institutions, announce the college vacancy, and request these individuals to refer qualified candidates for consideration. Such contacts generally refer other candidates and often apply for the position themselves.

Advertising. Classified advertising is another primary source of employment recruitment. Through careful selection of the media and its circulation audience, including professional and trade publications such as the *Chronicle of Higher Education*, a college can obtain maximum results from affirmative action recruitment efforts. However, advertising can be expensive; thus, care should be exercised in selecting the vehicle.

There are three basic types of advertising formats in publications: (1) classified, in which the type size is standard, and the advertisement is in paragraph form, and the charge is generally by word or by line;

(2) classified display, in which the type size is standard and the advertisement is in paragraph form, using standard column width with a border around it, and is usually charged by column inches (column width times the length in inches); and (3) display, in which choice of type style and format is provided, with a border around the advertisement, and the charge is by column inches. (See Exhibit 1D.)

Other Sources. These include social service and religious organizations, churches, and college placement offices. Such sources are inexpensive and can also assist the college in its affirmative action recruitment efforts. Billboards in the community or advertising space on buses or taxicabs should not be overlooked; they provide considerable exposure for limited cost. Administrators should be alert to any other potential recruitment sources available.

Preemployment Inquiries and Screening

Preemployment information from applicants is generally solicited on employment applications and during preemployment interviews. Such inquiries have undergone drastic changes in the last ten years, since many that were used previously are now illegal because they are discriminatory or not job-related. The illegality of certain questions applies whether they are presented on a written employment application or orally during an interview. (See Exhibit 1E.)

Employment Applications. Most employment applications can be limited to one or two pages; no questions should be used that do not relate to the job applied for. Employment applications generally include the following major areas: (1) personal information; (2) employment history; (3) knowledge, skills, and abilities; (4) references; and (5) a general statement concerning misrepresentation of information and the fact that this could result in disqualification or dismissal from employment. (See Exhibits $1F_1$ and $1F_2$.)

Most employers struggle with the perennial problem of keeping application files up-to-date. There is no foolproof method for this, but there are several ways to increase the accuracy of the files. One is to request that applicants notify the college if they are no longer interested in employment there. Also, one may indicate that an application will be maintained as active for only two or three months. At the expiration of that period, a postcard can be mailed to the applicant advising that the card must be returned or a telephone call placed to the college if the applicant is still interested in employment there.

A college should retain application forms for at least three years. This period conforms to the records retention regulations of most federal and state agencies. However, colleges should review the records retention requirements of their state, county, or municipal jurisdiction in order to comply. Application forms must be retained indefinitely if a complaint is filed by an applicant.

Affirmative Action Information. Any college with an affirmative action plan may be required to collect data on the sex and race of applicants. This information can be obtained legally during the preemployment process by two methods: (1) visual observation or (2) solicitation of voluntary information from the employee (orally or in writing). There are advantages and disadvantages to both methods. The visual method tends to be less accurate, but it does not require seeking the information directly from the applicant. While the second approach is usually more accurate, some employees may be reluctant to volunteer information. However, many employers prefer the latter method. (See Exhibit 1G.)

Whichever method is used, the information gained must be kept separate from the general preemployment information and must not be available to those responsible for making the employment decision. Since most central employment functions of colleges serve only as screening agencies, with final selection made by the hiring department, this information is best solicited and maintained in the central employment office.

Screening and Interviewing. As a general rule, the more exhaustive the screening process, the more likely the best qualified candidate available will be matched to a job vacancy. It is recommended that initial screening of applicants be assigned to the centralized employment function. If the individual assigned this responsibility uses appropriate interviewing techniques, and screens against the position description, unqualified applicants can be eliminated and qualified candidates can be referred to campus offices and departments for further screening. Questions asked during interviews are subject to the same legal constraints as are those appearing on the employment application form. (See Exhibit 1H.)

Testing. Prior to establishment of the EEOC guidelines and the U.S. Supreme Court's subsequent Griggs decision, the testing of applicants was a widespread screening device used by most employers. Since then, however, although testing has not been outlawed, technical validation criteria have been established for all testing. As with the use of minimum qualifications, any test used as a screening or selection device must demonstrate or predict successful job performance. Specific details for test validation may be found in the *Uniform Guidelines on Employee Selection Procedures* issued in 1978 by the EEOC, the federal agency charged with enforcement of the Civil Rights Act. The concept of "adverse impact" (see p. 6) is particularly applicable to testing.

The validation requirements have prompted most employers to eliminate testing altogether or to limit it to skills testing, such as typing and shorthand. Aptitude tests and tests of general mental ability are some of the most difficult to validate and should be used only after proper validation. It is recommended that small colleges consider administering only skills testing because of the high costs associated with validation requirements. A basic skills testing program is a valuable service for departments seeking clerical applicants, but it should be administered centrally to insure uniform test administration and evaluation standards.

Physical Examinations. Preemployment physical examinations are still widely used, particularly for occupations involving physical labor, such as custodian or groundskeeper. Since colleges are liable for worker's compensation, sick leave, and sometimes disability insurance, it is prudent to determine whether a prospective employee can physically perform a job.

Many employers have expressed concern that an initial reading of the Section 504 regulations concerning the handicapped seems to indicate that they prohibit preemployment physical examinations. However, such examinations are *not* prohibited by the 504 regulations, provided that they are administered to all applicants and not only to those who appear to have a physical disability.

A literal reading of the 504 regulations suggests that physical examinations cannot be administered selectively by occupation, such as for jobs involving physical labor but not for clerical positions. Common sense, however, establishes a distinct difference between the two occupational groups. Each institution must decide this issue for itself, but it seems reasonable that a justifiable case can be presented for selection based on occupation; it could remain for the courts to ultimately decide this issue.

Colleges with health center facilities have a definite cost advantage in administering physical examinations. If these are properly administered to applicants prior to employment, many worker's compensation and disability insurance benefits can be saved.

Reference Checks. Both employment and personal reference checks are another step in a thorough preemployment screening procedure. Employment references, although not always entirely accurate, are generally the most reliable and revealing check on an applicant's work experience, work habits, and work traits. The reliability rate of these references is probably close to 60% or 70%, a figure that also relates to the solicitor's frequent failure to ask pertinent questions.

Former employers are often reluctant to write about or even discuss a former employee unless they know personally the solicitor of such information. A cardinal rule of employment and personnel professionals is to say very little in responding to references and not to offer information that is not solicited. More reliable references usually can be obtained if the reference check is conducted by telephone, since nothing is committed to writing, especially if the solicitor and former employer are personally acquainted. If the former employer is not known personally, employment references ideally would be obtained from the person who had direct supervision over the applicant. However, if this person is unavailable or prefers not to provide a reference, an alternative approach may be required. A representative of the personnel function should contact a person in a similar position at the applicant's present or former place of employment. Personnel representatives tend to be candid with one another because of the inherent expectation that shared reference information will be given confidential treatment.

Although the latter approach—through the personnel representative—has the disadvantage of not receiving information that is obtained from direct observation of the applicant, it can still be valuable. Most personnel offices maintain written performance evaluations on all employees; these can be consulted by the company personnel representative for reference information.

Personal references also have their place in the employment process, although a favorable bias is usually inherent, since the applicant has selected the individual from whom the reference is to be solicited. Occasionally, a personal reference check will result in a candid, even negative, recommendation. The reliability of personal references can be enhanced if the questions are carefully phrased for a written check or carefully prepared in advance for a telephone check. (See Exhibits $1I_1$ and $1I_2$.) In telephone reference checks, one may "read between the lines," noting voice inflections, pauses, and so on. (See Exhibits $1I_1$ and $1J_2$.)

Supervisors of the employing department may be used to solicit references on applicants for technical positions, since they are usually better qualified to seek and ultimately evaluate technical information received.

Security and Background Checks. These checks, including credit checks, are no longer used as much as previously. This decline can be traced to various laws that have restricted the availability of such information, and to other laws that require the disclosure of public records information. Furthermore, in most occupations, evidence of a conviction cannot in and of itself serve as a bar against employment. For example, conviction for embezzlement might legitimately disqualify an applicant for a position as cashier, but not necessarily for a position as clerk-typist or secretary.

Campus security can verify local police records and sometimes those within a state, but they cannot, for employment screening purposes, tap the federal National Crime Information Center records. Credit references from a credit bureau or other service can be obtained legally, provided applicants are apprised on the application for employment that credit references will be sought. If information generated from these reports becomes a basis for disqualification for employment, the applicant has a right to know the name and address of the firm that produced the report and, under the Fair Credit Reporting Act, the applicant can demand to see a copy of the report from the company producing it. A further development is that employers can no longer discharge an employee for one wage garnishment order.

With the escalating cost of purchasing credit reports, many employers have discontinued the use of such checks. Nevertheless, it is recommended that police checks be conducted on applicants for key administrative positions, particularly on persons being considered for employment in the financial areas of the institution.

Employment Referral

When the office responsible for applicant screening has completed its preliminary activities, three to five qualified applicants should be referred to the hiring department. Fewer than three applicants will not provide the department with a sufficient number for analysis and comparison of the applicants' backgrounds and qualifications. However, an initial referral of more than five applicants suggests that preliminary screening was not sufficiently selective or that the supply of qualified applicants far exceeds the demands.

Occasionally, there are instances when more than five referrals should be made; for example, to achieve affirmative action objectives. However, this is not cost-effective because the hiring department must then, in effect, duplicate the screening function. If a department is dissatisfied with all applicants who are referred initially, additional referrals can be made later.

Certain basic information should accompany the referral of an applicant to a department. This includes the application for employment for new employees and, if a skills testing program is maintained, the results of these tests. Employment and personal references, if already solicited, may sometimes be referred to the department as additional information; however, the confidentiality of a reference may be breached by referral.

An acceptable alternative is to indicate that references are on file in the central employment office for review. This preserves confidentiality by making references available to authorized persons only, on a "need to know" basis. At the same time departments can be advised orally of any negative reference information on a referred applicant if the negative information has not already disqualified the applicant from employment. This method also permits a judgment to be made regarding the validity of the reference information.

Some colleges have formalized the applicant referral process with a personnel or applicant referral form. (See Exhibits $1K_1$ and $1K_2$.) In most colleges, the employing department assumes a primary responsibility for insuring that employment decisions have been made in conformity with equal employment opportunity laws and the institution's affirmative action plan. The applicant referral form is often used as a means of obtaining certification from the employing department that the decision was made in consonance with these principles. A copy of the completed form is returned to the centralized employment office and filed with related referral information on that position vacancy.

If a written referral form is not used, an alternative retention method must be designed to maintain the record of applicants referred. This information must be maintained in the event that an unsuccessful applicant files a discrimination charge with a compliance agency. Position vacancy referral files (just as applications for employment) should be maintained for a minimum of three years, or indefinitely if a discrimination charge is filed. The referral of present employees to position vacancies is discussed in the section "Transfers and Promotions."

Selection of Successful Candidate

Following the selection of a prospective employee by the department, an offer of employment should be made by a representative of the central employment office. There are several reasons why the offer should come from this office: (1) most offers are communicated orally and should be followed up in writing by the person who made the oral offer, incorporating any conditions of employment; (2) if physical examinations are required by the institution, they generally take place at this point in the process and are coordinated by the employment office (also, the applicant should be advised that the successful completion of this examination is a condition of employment); (3) consonant with equal pay considerations, beginning salaries must be consistent with those being paid to current employees who have similar qualifications and are performing similar jobs, and departments usually do not have this information.

The central employment office also should notify the unsuccessful applicants that they have not been selected. These applicants should be encouraged to retain an interest in employment with the institution. Tactful oral or written communication can go a long way toward insuring continued interest in employment and in cultivating good community relations for the college. (See Exhibits $1L_1$–$1L_5$.)

Postemployment Process

The postemployment process begins when a selected candidate has accepted an offer of employment and is placed on the payroll. Other procedures of postemployment include gathering further information and conducting a probationary period.

Appointment Processing

If the selected applicant accepts an offer of employment, he or she is placed on the payroll and enrolled in benefit programs. The central employment office should authorize the appointment and route necessary documents to the payroll office. While this process varies among colleges, certain basic information is required for all appointments and an "appointment form" is an efficient method for processing these, whether the payroll system is manual or computerized. If the payroll system or the personnel records system is computerized, the appointment form can also serve as the source document for such records. A multi-use "change of status" form can be used for appointment processing as well as for other employment steps. (See Exhibits $1M_1$ and $1M_2$.)

Postemployment Information. Many inquiries considered illegal during the preemployment process are legal under postemployment processing. Certain information, such as that concerning race and citizenship, must be maintained by employers under affirmative action and equal employment opportunity laws. Such information is needed for reports such as the EEO-6 form and new-hire data for affirmative action plans. This information should be maintained separately from basic personnel files. (See Exhibits 1N.)

Probationary Period

In most colleges, a new employee serves a probationary or trial period. This may vary from a few weeks for relatively simple, repetitive jobs to a year or longer for highly technical, professional jobs. It is recommended that some reasonable, predetermined trial period be required for new employees, based on the time needed to learn the duties and responsibilities of the job. It should be stated in writing, preferably in the conditions of employment or college rules and regulations, that dismissal can occur during this time based solely on the decision of the employer.

A new employee should be advised that the probationary period is also an opportunity to determine whether he or she finds the job satisfactory. The employee should receive adequate instruction on how to perform the job and should be encouraged to ask questions. Periodic evaluation of a new employee should be carried out by the supervisor during this time and the employee should be apprised of his or her progress.

Prior to the expiration of probation, a supervisor should conscientiously and objectively determine whether an employee should be retained. Generally speaking, an employee is on "best behavior" during this work test period; thus, if work quality, quantity, or habits are not acceptable, the employee should be dismissed. Obviously, these decisions should not be arbitrary or capricious. (Performance evaluations are explained in detail in Chapter 4.)

Transfers and Promotions

Effective transfer and promotion policies, which provide opportunities for employee growth, are essential to a sound personnel program. Absence of such opportunities is often a major factor contributing to poor employee morale. While employers may boast that they practice promotion from within, an objective survey among employees could reveal the opposite view. Further, so much is said about the mobility of today's work force that "job hopping" is accepted as a product of modern society, and some employers may use this as an excuse for employee turnover.

Contemporary management practices have resulted in job enrichment programs designed to make jobs more interesting and challenging. However, many of these programs were developed because of growing employer frustration with employee turnover or high absenteeism, rather than because of the need to make programs more effective.

The challenge to develop an effective promotion program is complex, particularly in a college, where departments and offices often function with more or less autonomy. However, if employees lack real promotion and transfer opportunities, they will seek employment elsewhere or consider unionization. Colleges must attempt to cultivate positive attitudes toward promotion and transfer among their supervisory ranks. When implementing a "promotion from within" program, one difficult policy decision is whether a *well* qualified internal candidate should be selected over an external candidate who may be the *best* qualified for the job. The adoption of clear-cut policies in critical areas such as this is necessary to the development of effective personnel programs.

Promotions from within usually carry a test period analogous to the probationary period. Department heads may be reluctant to accept a present employee over an outside applicant unless the opportunity is provided to test the employee on the job. A common procedure provides that if an employee moves to a higher-level job, but is not successful, he or she can return to the old job, to one in the same classification, or to a

similarly classified position. A small college may have difficulty following this procedure if an appropriate vacancy does not exist to which a
promoted employee could return. (Alternative programs for developing
career paths by promotion from within are described in Chapter 4.)

Job Posting

Qualified employees should be encouraged to apply for vacancies in
the college that afford opportunities for promotion. An effective means
of notifying employees of vacancies beyond the entry level is to use a
"job posting" system, which communicates news of job vacancies
through bulletin boards, "dial-a-job" recordings, or other internal communications. These should encourage applications from employees who
meet the minimum qualifications of the posted job. The central employment office staff must exercise considerable judgment in referring
qualified employees for the vacant position. An ideal "promotion from
within" system would restrict application for vacancies to current
employees only for the first week. However, this could be contrary to the
institution's affirmative action plan unless the current work force reflects
proper utilization of protected classes.

Since members of protected classes are underrepresented in the work
forces of many colleges, simultaneous internal and external announce-
ments of position vacancies generally are required to meet affirmative action program guidelines. The job-posting system has the advantage of
apprising everyone of a vacancy when it occurs, thus placing the responsibility on the employee to pursue the opportunity. (See Exhibit 1"O".)

Separation

Employees may leave the employ of a college by various means, including resignation, discharge, retirement, and death. Resignation is the
primary method of leaving employment.

Resignation

Colleges should require written resignations, preferably on an institutional form. There are three primary reasons for obtaining a written
statement of voluntary separation: (1) it avoids misunderstanding concerning the reason for separation, (2) it can be an important document in
challenging an unemployment compensation claim, and (3) it can be an
important document if a discrimination charge is filed by a former employee who alleges that he or she was discharged or forced to resign. The
use of oral, rather than written, resignation is unwise, and could prove
costly to the institution. (See Exhibit 1P.)

Discharge

A notice of discharge should always be presented in writing to an employee, preferably by registered letter to the employee's last known home address. The written notice may follow an oral notification of discharge and should explain the reasons for discharge, preferably citing the college work rules or regulation that prompted it. Letters of discharge should be succinct and clear, and all such notices should be processed through the central employment office to insure consistency of format. Centralized processing also maintains uniformity in application of other disciplinary actions, such as "letter of warning" and "disciplinary suspension without pay" (see Chapter 5).

Separation Process

All separations should be channeled through the central employment office, which should use a check list or other form to insure that all steps are taken for the efficient separation of employees. An institution's insurance programs may contain a conversion provision for direct payment of premiums to the carrier subsequent to employment; if so, this option can be communicated and sometimes acted on prior to separation. College property maintained by employees, such as keys, uniforms, handbooks, and identification cards, can be deposited at the employment office, or verification can be obtained that these items have been returned to the appropriate office.

Exit Interview

Employee turnover is costly to any employer, but particularly to colleges, which are labor-intensive. The resignation process can be an opportunity to determine why employees are leaving, so that any necessary corrective action may be taken; the "exit interview" is widely used in higher education for this purpose. An exit interview or exit interview questionnaire elicits the departing employee's reasons for leaving and includes an evaluation of wages paid, benefits, and working conditions. (See Exhibits $1Q_1$ and $1Q_2$.)

The exit interview can provide valuable information that might not be obtained otherwise. Such interviews ideally should be conducted by a representative of the employment office who is skilled in interviewing. Since the employment office is generally responsible for assisting the employee with procedures such as the conversion of insurance benefits, this process can easily be combined with the exit interview.

Staff Turnover

Staff turnover provides an accepted measure of the effectiveness of screening, selection, and placement of employees. Although not totally representative of these techniques, turnover can indicate faulty processes. Among different formulas to determine rate of staff turnover, the simplest is to divide the average number of employees during a given period into the total number of separations. Most colleges, under this method, should have a turnover rate of approximately 15% to 20% annually. (This can vary according to geographical areas and other factors.) If the turnover rate for a year exceeds 30%, there may be a serious problem with screening, placement, wages, benefits, working conditions, or promotional opportunities. This method for calculating turnover rate is recommended because it is easy to compute and to read.

Exhibit 1A$_1$

Position Control Card				
Employment Date	Name	Budget Approval	Termination Date	Comment

Area: _____

Title _____   Code No. _____   Position No. _____

(This sample is intended for use as a 5 × 8 card in a visible index system.)

Exhibit 1A$_2$

Full-Time	Part-Time	Temp.	Perm.	Position Control Card				Status	Position Number
				INCUMBENT					

Employee's Name	Date Employed	Salary	Date Terminated	Remarks

Classification	Date	Classification	Date

Department

(Additional information on the incumbent can be maintained on the reverse side of the card.)

Exhibit 1B

Employee Control Form

Name		Social Security No.	Birth Date		
			Sex Male Female		
Address		Phone	Height Weight		
			Citizen Yes No		
			Marital S M W D		
Physical Restriction		Military: Branch	Discharge Reserve		
Education: Elementary 4 · 5 · 6 · 7 · 8		High 9 · 10 · 11 · 12 Other:			

College	School	Date(s)	Degree/Date	Major

Dependents	Birth Year	Relation	Dependents	Birth Year	Relation	Med-Surg:	Cov.	Waiver
						Life: Cert. No.		Waiver
						LTD:		Waiver
						TRS:		
						ORP: Carrier		Tax Def.
Emergency: Name			Relation			TDA:		Date
Address			Phone					

(reverse side of card)   **EMPLOYMENT HISTORY**

Date	Action/Code	Position	Job Code	Department	Rate			
					HR	MO	ANN	OPT
			(add lines as necessary)					

		REVIEW DATE											P/S	CIT	SEX
	E	YR	JAN	FEB	MAR	APR	MAY	JUN	JUL	AUG	SEP	OCT	NOV	DEC

Exhibit 1C$_1$

Personnel Requisition
SUPPORTIVE OPERATING STAFF

Department	
Date of Request	
Department Chairperson	

<table>
<tr><td rowspan="5">Budgetary</td><td>Job Title:</td><td>Full-time</td><td colspan="2">Part-time</td><td colspan="2">Temporary</td></tr>
<tr><td>Replacing:</td><td>Date Needed:</td><td colspan="3">Incumbent's Termination Date</td></tr>
<tr><td>Approximate Salary Recommended</td><td colspan="2">Account Title</td><td colspan="2">Budget Account No.</td></tr>
<tr><td colspan="5">The recommended salary for this is different from the normal hiring rate position because:</td></tr>
</table>

<table>
<tr><td rowspan="2">Replacement</td><td colspan="2">If this request is for a replacement, does the following apply?</td><td>Yes</td><td>No</td></tr>
<tr><td colspan="4">
1. Alternate methods of accomplishing work have been examined and elimination of this position is not warranted?
2. Has any change occurred in the funding which initially supported this position?
3. Is work force properly organized for maximum production?
4. Is a fully skilled person required, or can one with basic skills be trained on the job for economy purposes?

No commitment may be made to any current or prospective employee until all appropriate approvals are secured.
</td></tr>
</table>

New Position	
	☐ New Position ☐ Summer Help ☐ Other
	The number of supportive operating staff currently authorized to support the function of this department is _____.
	No new positions, regardless of the funding sources, may be filled and no commitment may be made to any current or prospective employee until all appropriate approvals are secured.

Duties, Qualifications	
	Typical duties, responsibilities, qualifications, justification, and additional remarks. Please be as specific as possible when completing this section.
	Remarks:

<table>
<tr><td rowspan="2">Approval</td><td>Dean/Director</td><td>Date</td><td>Controller</td><td>Date</td></tr>
<tr><td>Vice President for Finance & Management</td><td>Date</td><td>Director of Personnel Services</td><td>Date</td></tr>
</table>

Routing	
	Route copies as follows: Originator: Retain canary copy and forward pink and white copies in sealed envelope to your division head—i.e., Provost, Dean/Director, or Vice President for Finance & Management, as appropriate. Provost, Dean/Director, or Vice President for Finance & Management: Approve and retain pink copy and forward white copy to Controller in a sealed envelope. Controller: After approval as to availability of funds, forward white copy to Personnel Services in a sealed envelope.

Exhibit 1C$_2$

PERSONNEL REQUISITION

1. REQUESTED BY   2. DEPARTMENT   3. DATE

_____   _____   _____

4. JOB TITLE   5. DATE NEEDED

6.   ◯ PERMANENT   ◯ TEMPORARY → IF TEMP., HOW LONG?

7. BRIEF OUTLINE OF MAJOR DUTIES

8. EDUCATION NEEDED

9. EXPERIENCE NEEDED

10. SPECIAL SKILLS NEEDED

11. WHO WILL SUPERVISE THIS EMPLOYEE?

12. WHOM WILL THIS EMPLOYEE SUPERVISE?

IF NEW POSITION, COMPLETE THE FOLLOWING

13. POSITION FUNDED BY   ◯   ◯ GRANT FUNDS

                                        BUDGET CODE

GENERAL COMMENTS

APPROVAL

TO INSURE PROMPT ACTION ON YOUR REQUIREMENTS, COMPLETE ALL NECESSARY INFORMATION AS BRIEFLY AND CLEARLY AS POSSIBLE AND FORWARD TO THE PERSONNEL DEPARTMENT.	SIGNATURE	DATE

Exhibit 1D

How to Write a Classified Advertisement

The following article was prepared by James M. Elliott, of the Pennsylvania State University, for the "How-to" series published by the College and University Personnel Association.

These questions should be answered before placing newspaper advertising:

1. What heading (job title) and content shall I use to attract a person with the type of background—that is, skills, experience, education, and other qualifications—I am seeking?
2. Where shall I advertise?
3. When shall I advertise?
4. How should the advertisement look?

What Heading Shall I Use?

Perhaps you're asked to recruit an instructor to teach the repair and operation of electronic equipment, and someone with experience as an electronic specialist would be fine for this position. Such an individual would hardly give a second glance at an advertisement titled "Instructor," but he or she would certainly read one headed "Electronics Technician." The official job title can be clarified later in the advertisement, in a telephone conversation, or by letter. At times it may be desirable or necessary to cross-reference an advertisement under several other job titles to reach the broadest audience of related backgrounds.

Experts say that the earlier in the "help wanted" section an advertisement is placed, the better. (Advertisements usually are listed alphabetically.) Thus, if you are looking for a project coordinator for your maintenance department, the advertisement might be set up as follows:

Administrative
PROJECT COORDINATOR
(Maintenance)
[copy]_____

Using the word "administrative" first places the advertisement in the "A" section.

How Should I Word the Advertisement (Content)?

Don't do too much screening with an advertisement. For example, it could be a mistake to state that an applicant must have at least five years of experience. Perhaps a reader has only three and one-half years of related experience, but the experience is especially good and may be adequate for the job. This person should not be deterred from answering the advertisement through too firm a limitation on qualifications. More detailed screening can be done through correspondence. However, the advertisement should mention any *specific* qualifications, such as "must be Certified Public Accountant."

Don't try to sell what everyone else has to offer. Benefits, such as retirement program and paid vacation, can be mentioned. But perhaps you also offer benefits which your competitors do not, such as educational privileges for the employee and his or her family, or extra paid vacation at Christmas. Be sure to emphasize such items. Also, you may use phrases such as "pleasant campus atmosphere," "many cultural activities," etc. Make the advertisement conversational; try to make the reader *want* to respond. Remember, you're selling something. So use a sales approach.

How Should the Advertisement Look?

First, the heading should be in fairly bold type to attract the reader's attention. The body of the advertisement can be in regular (agate) type. If the reader is interested, the advertisement will be read, regardless of its size. If competition is keen for the talents you're seeking, it may be necessary to use a "display" advertisement to make it more distinctive.

Where Shall I Advertise?

Consider the areas where a person with the type of background you are seeking is most likely to be found. For example, areas where large aircraft manufacturers are located typically are good sources of persons with engineering skills.

Distance from the institution should be kept in mind when considering advertising media. An eastern institution may have difficulty negotiating with an applicant on the West Coast because of problems in interviewing, relocation, and so forth.

Generally, urban newspapers produce the largest responses. Also, such newspapers generally cover more than the metropolitan areas. However, only one good applicant reading a "small town" newspaper is necessary to fill an opening. A number of advertisements can be placed in smaller newspapers for a price comparable to that of one advertisement in a metropolitan newspaper.

When Shall I Advertise?

Sundays are best for urban newspapers. These are distributed to homes throughout the state and often they include a featured classified section on employment. However, the daily urban newspapers often do not carry classified advertisements in their rural editions. For daily newspapers, the earlier in the week the better for placing advertisements. Job seekers do not seem to be as active in their search toward the end of the week.

Fair Employment Practice Laws

The federal government and most states have laws that prohibit discriminatory advertising. These laws make it illegal for "help wanted" advertisements to specify race, creed, national origin, sex, or age (unless sex or age is a *bona fide occupational qualification* for the job advertised). The inclusion of the following statement at the end of the advertisement is suggested: "An Equal Opportunity/Affirmative Action Employer."

A Sample Advertisement

Personnel Assistant

Opening at _____ College in the employee personnel department. Experience in personnel work or related areas preferred, plus bachelor's degree or equivalent. Many liberal benefits, including educational privileges for you and your family. Pleasant college town in a scenic part of the state, with excellent hunting, fishing, camping, and other recreational facilities. Write to: (address).

An Equal Opportunity/Affirmative Action Employer

Advertisement Check List

1. Title: Does it communicate?
2. What is the job?
3. Where is it?
4. Who should apply? (special skills, experience, etc.)
5. Selling points (what makes you an attractive employer?)
6. How does one apply for the job?
7. Does the advertisement violate any federal or state antidiscrimination legislation?

Exhibit 1E

PREEMPLOYMENT INQUIRY GUIDE

Purpose of the Guide

There are a variety of federal laws and executive orders requiring equal employment opportunity and affirmative action. Under these laws certain practices relating to employment on the part of employers, labor unions, employment agencies, and others are considered illegal if such practices discriminate against persons because of race, sex, age, religion, color, handicap, ancestry, or arrest and court record. The scope of these laws has been expanded by recent court decisions.

These laws and court rulings make it necessary for employers and others who hire workers to take precautions concerning the content of their employment application forms as well as questions sometimes asked of job applicants. This guide is provided to assist in understanding and applying the law, and to help avoid asking questions in the pre-employment process that would give potentially prejudicial information.

It should be understood clearly that **this guide is not a complete definition of what can and cannot be asked of applicants.** It is illustrative and attempts to answer the questions most frequently asked concerning the law. It is hoped that in most cases the given rules, either directly or by analogy, will guide all personnel involved in the preemployment processes of recruiting, interviewing, and selection. This guide pertains only to inquiries, advertisements, etc., directed to all applicants **prior to employment.** Information required for records such as race, sex, and number of dependents may be requested after the applicant is on the payroll provided such information is not used for any subsequent discrimination, as in upgrading or layoff.

Federal laws are not intended to prohibit employers from obtaining sufficient job-related information about applicants, as long as the questions do not elicit information that could be used for discriminatory purposes. Applicants should not be encouraged to volunteer information forbidden by law. These laws do not restrict the rights of employers to define qualifications necessary for satisfactory job performance, but require that standards of qualifications for hiring be applied equally to all persons considered for employment.

It is recognized that the mere routine adherence to law will not accomplish the results intended by the courts and Congress. Employment discrimination can be eliminated only if the laws and regulations are followed in the spirit in which they were conceived. This guide can assist efforts to insure equal employment opportunity at any college.

PREEMPLOYMENT INQUIRY GUIDE

Subject	Permissible Inquiries	Inquiries That Must Be Avoided
1. Name	"Have you worked for this company under a different name?" "Is any additional information relative to change of name, use of an assumed name or nickname necessary to enable a check on your work and educational record? If yes, explain."	Inquiries about the name that would indicate applicant's lineage, ancestry, national origin or descent. Inquiry into previous name of applicant where it has been changed by court order or otherwise. Indicate: Miss, Mrs., Ms.
2. Marital and Family Status	Whether applicant can meet specified work schedules or has activities, commitments, or responsibilities that may hinder the meeting of work attendance requirements. Inquiries, made to males and females alike, as to a duration of stay on job or anticipated absences.	Any inquiry indicating whether an applicant is married, single, divorced, engaged, etc. Number and age of children. Information on child-care arrangements. Any questions concerning pregnancy. Any similar question that directly or indirectly results in limitation of job opportunity in any way.
3. Age	If a minor, require proof of age in the form of a work permit or a certificate of age. Require proof of age by birth certificate after being hired. Inquiry as to whether or not the applicant meets the minimum age requirements as set by law and indication that, on hiring, proof of age must be submitted in the form of a birth certificate or other forms of proof of age. If age is a legal requirement: "If hired, can you furnish proof of age?" or statement that hire is subject to verification of age. Inquiry as to whether or not an applicant is younger than the employer's regular retirement age.	Requirement that applicant state age or date of birth. Requirement that applicant produce proof of age in the form of a birth certificate or baptismal record. (The Age Discrimination in Employment Act of 1967 forbids discrimination against persons between the ages of 40 and 70.)
4. Handicaps	For employers subject to the provisions of the Rehabilitation Act of 1973, applicants may be "invited" to indicate how and to what extent they are handicapped. The employer must indicate to applicants that: 1) compliance with the invitation is voluntary; 2) the information is being sought only to remedy discrimination or provide opportunities for the handicapped;	The Rehabilitation Act of 1973 forbids employers from asking job applicants general questions about whether they are handicapped or asking them about the nature and severity of their handicaps. An employer must be prepared to prove that any physical and mental requirements for a job are due to "business necessity"

	Permissible Inquiries	Inquiries That Must Be Avoided
	3) the information will be kept confidential; and 4) refusing to provide the information will not result in adverse treatment. All applicants can be asked if they are able to carry out all necessary job assignments and perform them in a safe manner.	and the safe performance of the job. Except in cases where undue hardship can be proven, employers must make "reasonable accommodations" for the physical and mental limitations of an employee or applicant. "Reasonable accommodation" includes alteration of duties, alteration of physical setting, and provision of aids.
5. Sex	Inquiry as to sex or restriction of employment to one sex is permissible only where a **bona fide occupational qualification** exists. (This BFOQ exception is interpreted very narrowly by the courts and EEOC.) The burden of proof rests on the employer to prove that the BFOQ does exist and that **all** members of the affected class are incapable of performing the job.	Sex of applicant. Any other inquiry which would indicate sex. Sex is **not** a BFOQ because a job involves physical labor (such as heavy lifting) beyond the capacity of **some** women, nor can employment be restricted just because the job is traditionally labeled "men's work" or "women's work." Sex cannot be used as a factor for determining whether or not an applicant will be satisfied in a particular job. Avoid questions concerning applicant's height or weight unless you can prove they are necessary requirements for the job to be performed.
6. Race or Color	General distinguishing physical characteristics, such as scars.	Applicant's race. Color of applicant's skin, eyes, hair, or other questions directly or indirectly indicating race or color.
7. Address or Duration of Residence	Applicant's address. Inquiry into place and length of current and previous addresses, e.g., "How long a resident of this state or city?"	Specific inquiry into foreign addresses which would indicate national origin. Names or relationship of persons with whom applicant resides. Whether applicant owns or rents home.
8. Birthplace	"After employment (if employed by this institution), can you submit a birth certificate or other proof of U.S. citizenship?"	Birthplace of applicant. Birthplace of applicant's parents, spouse, or other relatives. Requirement that applicant submit a birth certificate or naturalization or baptismal record before employment. Any other inquiry into national origin.

	Lawful	Unlawful
9. Religion	An applicant may be advised concerning normal hours and days of work required by the job to avoid possible conflict with religious or other personal convictions.	Applicant's religious denomination or affiliation, church, parish, pastor, or religious holidays observed. Applicants may not be told that any particular religious groups are required to work on their religious holidays. Any inquiry to indicate or identify religious denomination or customs.
10. Military Record	Type of education and experience in service as it relates to a particular job.	Type of discharge.
11. Photograph	Indicate that this may be required after hiring for identification.	Requirement that applicant affix a photograph to his or her application. Request that applicant, at his or her option, submit photograph. Requirement of photograph after interview but before hiring.
12. Citizenship	"Are you a citizen of the United States?" "If you are not a U.S. citizen, have you the legal right to remain permanently in the U.S.?" "Do you intend to remain permanently in the U.S.?" "If not a citizen, are you prevented from lawfully becoming employed because of visa or immigration status?" Statement that, if hired, applicant may be required to submit proof of citizenship.	"Of what country are you a citizen?" Whether applicant or his or her parents or spouse are naturalized or native-born U.S. citizens. Date when applicant or parents or spouse acquired U.S. citizenship. Requirement that applicant produce his or her naturalization papers. Whether applicant's parents or spouse are citizens of the U.S.
13. Ancestry or National Origin	Languages applicant reads, speaks, or writes fluently. (If another language is necessary to perform the job.)	Inquiries into applicant's lineage, ancestry, national origin, descent, birthplace, or mother tongue. National origin of applicant's parents or spouse.
14. Education	Applicant's academic, vocational, or professional education; school attended. Inquiry into language skills such as reading, speaking, and writing foreign languages.	Any inquiry asking specifically the nationality, racial, or religious affiliation of a school. Inquiry as to how foreign language ability was acquired.

	Permissible Inquiries	Inquiries That Must Be Avoided
15. Experience	Applicant's work experience, including names and addresses of previous employers, dates of employment, reasons for leaving, salary history. Other countries visited.	
16. Conviction, Arrest, and Court Record	Inquiry into actual **convictions** which relate reasonably to fitness to perform a particular job. (A conviction is a court ruling where the party is **found guilty** as charged. An arrest is merely the apprehending or detaining of the person to answer the **alleged crime**.)	Any inquiry relating to arrests. Ask or check into a person's arrest, court, or conviction record if not **substantially related** to functions and responsibilities of the particular job in question.
17. Relatives	Names of applicant's relatives already employed by this company. Names and addresses of parents or guardian of minor applicant.	Name or address of any relative of adult applicant, other than those employed by this company.
18. Notice in Case of Emergency	Name and address of persons to be notified in case of accident or emergency.	Name and address of **relatives** to be notified in case of accident or emergency.
19. Organizations	Inquiry into the organizations of which an applicant is a member providing the name or character of the organization does not reveal the race, religion, color, or ancestry of the membership. "List all professional organizations to which you belong. What offices are held?"	"List all organizations, clubs, societies, and lodges to which you belong." The names of organizations to which the applicant belongs if such information would indicate through character or name the race, religion, color, or ancestry of the membership.
20. References	By whom were you referred for a position here? Names of persons willing to provide professional and/or character references for applicant.	Require the submission of a religious reference. Request reference from applicant's pastor.
21. Miscellaneous	Notice to applicants that any misstatements or omissions of material facts in the application may be cause for dismissal.	

Any inquiry should be avoided which, although not specifically listed among the above, is designed to elicit information as to race, color, ancestry, age, sex, religion, handicap, or arrest and court record unless based upon a <u>bona fide occupational qualification.</u>

Exhibit 1F₁

Application For Employment

Please Read

AN EQUAL OPPORTUNITY EMPLOYER

Before completing this application, you are advised that work schedules and duties may be modified from time to time at the convenience of the college. You are further advised that alternate similar job functions may be assigned during those periods when school is not in session. Completion of this form indicates an acceptance of these conditions.

Please Print

Last Name	First	Middle	Soc. Sec. No.	

Address	No. & Street	City	State	Zip Code	Telephone

PERSONAL

Length of Time at Present Address	Previous Address

Notify in Emergency	Name

Address	Phone

Have You Any Functional Disabilities That Could Affect Your Performance in the Job You Have Applied For?

No. of Days Lost from Work in Past Year Due to Illness or Other Reasons.   Explain

Have You Been Convicted of a Serious Crime Within the Last Five Years? (A conviction record will not be a bar to employment, depending on such factors as your age at the time of the crime, seriousness of the crime, and nature of the crime in relation to the position you are applying for.)

JOB INTEREST

Position Desired	Salary Expected (Per Month)	Date Available

Other Positions for Which Qualified

Who Interested You in Us or Who Referred You to Us?

Name of Relatives Employed by College (Indicate Location Where Employed)

Have You Ever Been Employed by This College? If Yes, When & Where?	Have You Ever Applied for Employment With This College? If Yes, When & Where?

EDUCATION

Circle Highest Grade Completed in <u>Each</u> Category	High School 9 10 11 12		College 1 2 3 4	
Name & Location of High School	Course	Year Grad.	Class Rank	
Name & Location of College	Degree Major	Year Grad.	Class Rank	
Name & Location of Business, Apprentice or Vocational School	Course	Year Grad.	Class Rank	
Are You Studying Now?	What?		Where?	

Other Training or Skills: Typing wpm   Yrs. Experience   Shorthand wpm Yrs. Experience

Check (X) Any Equipment You Are Now Capable of Operating:

☐ Typewriter ☐ Dictaphone ☐ Key Punch Machine ☐ Adding Machine ☐ Calculating Machine
☐ Electronic Data Processing Equip. (Specify Type Below)   ☐ Other Machines (Specify Below)

MILITARY

Branch of U.S. Service	Service Schools or Special Experience

Selective Service Number & Classification	Local Board No. & Address	Reserve or National Guard Status

personnel practices

EMPLOYMENT HISTORY

List all employment for last ten years. Begin with most recent first and account for any lapses in employment.

Name of Employer	Address	Dates From To

Job Title	Department	Name of Supervisor

Describe Major Job Duties

Monthly Salary Starting Final	Reason For Leaving

Name of Employer	Address	Dates From To

Job Title	Department	Name of Supervisor

Describe Major Job Duties

Monthly Salary Starting Final	Reason For Leaving

Name of Employer	Address	Dates From To

Job Title	Department	Name of Supervisor

Describe Major Job Duties

Monthly Salary Starting Final	Reason For Leaving

May We Contact Your Present Employer?

REFERENCES

List the Names of Three Personal References Who Know You Well:
Do Not List Former Employers, Relatives or Close Friends.

Name	Street and City Address	Telephone	Occupation	How Long Has He or She Known You?

Remarks (Use This Space to Provide Any Additional Information You Feel Will Assist Us in Evaluating Your Qualifications For Employment).

I hereby certify that, to the best of my knowledge, the answers to the foregoing questions and statements are true and correct. If anything contained in this application is found to be untrue, I understand I will be subject to dismissal at anytime during my employment. I further understand that employment may be contingent upon my passing a physical examination to the satisfaction of the college medical examiner. If employment is obtained under this application I will comply with all rules and regulations of the college. I also authorize my former employers to release any information they may have regarding me. I understand this application is valid for one year only.

Signature of Applicant _____

Date _____

Do Not Write in this Space
Comments:

This college does not engage in discrimination in its programs, activities, and policies against students, prospective students, employees, or prospective employees, on account of race, color, religion, ethnic or national origin, age, personal handicap, or sex. Such policy is in compliance with the requirements of Titles VI and VII of the Civil Rights Act of 1964, Title IX of the Education Amendments of 1972, the Rehabilitation Act of 1973, and all other applicable federal, state, and local statutes, ordinances, and regulations.

Interviewed By: _____ Date: _____

employment

35

Exhibit 1F₂

Application for Employment

Date _____

Name _____ Social Security No. ___-___-_____
      Last   First   Middle Initial

Present Address _____ Telephone No. (___) _____
     No.   Street   City   State   Zip   Area Code

Person to be notified in case of accident or emergency_____
                                                     Name

_____   Telephone No. _____
                Address

Do you have any functional disabilities that could affect your performance in the job you have applied for?

_____

_____

Position(s) Applied For: _____ Date Available for Work_____

Would you work Full-Time___ Part-Time___ Specify days and hours if part-time_____

Where did you learn of this position?_____ Rate of pay expected_____

List any friends or relatives working for us_____
                              Name   Relationship

_____
                              Name   Relationship

Were you previously employed by us?___ If yes, when and in what capacity?_____

Have you been convicted of a serious crime within the last five years?___ If yes, explain_____
(A conviction record will not be a bar to employment, depending on such factors as your age at the time of the crime, seriousness of the crime, and nature of the crime in relation to the position you are applying for).

_____

_____

List activities and interests _____

_____

Indicate area of competency:

☐ Adding Machine	☐ Dictaphone	☐ Shorthand _____wpm
☐ Bookkeeping Machine	☐ Filing	☐ Switchboard
☐ Calculator	☐ Keypunch	☐ Typing _____wpm
☐ Computer	☐ Offset	☐ Other _____

Record of Education

School	Name and Address of School	Course of Study	How Many Years Attended	Circle Last Year Completed				Did You Graduate?	List Diploma or Degree
Elementary				5	6	7	8	☐ Yes ☐ No	
High				1	2	3	4	☐ Yes ☐ No	
College				1	2	3	4	☐ Yes ☐ No	
Other (Specify)				1	2	3	4	☐ Yes ☐ No	

Military Experience

Branch of Service: _____ Highest Rank Held: _____

List duties in the service including special training _____

Did you attend school while in the service?____ If yes, what course(s)? _____

Military Specialty _____

Personal References (Not Former Employers or Relatives)

Name and Occupation	Address	Phone Number	Years Known

List below all present and past employment, beginning with your most recent

Name and Address of Company and Type of Business	From		To		Describe the work you did	Weekly Starting Salary	Weekly Last Salary	Reason for Leaving	Name of Supervisor and Title
	Mo.	Yr.	Mo.	Yr.					
I									
II									
III									

[add space as desired]

Have you ever been bonded?_____ If yes, on what jobs?_____

May we contact the employers listed above?_____ If not, indicate by number which one(s) you do not wish us to contact _____

The facts set forth above in my application for employment are true and complete. I understand that if employed, false statements on this application shall be considered sufficient cause for dismissal.

_____
Signature of Applicant

Return application to:

It is the policy of this college not to discriminate on the basis of race, color, creed, sex, national origin, age, or mental or physical handicap of applicants. This is in compliance with Section 504 of the Rehabilitation Act of 1973 and with Title IX of the 1972 Education Amendments.

Applicant—Do not write on this page
For Interviewer's Use

Interviewer	Date	Comments

[add space as necessary]

For Test Administrator's Use

Tests Administered	Date	Raw Score	Rating	Comments And Interpretation

[add space as necessary]

Title/Position _____ Starting Date _____

Work Location _____ Rate/Range _____

Reference Check

*Position Number	Results Of Reference Check	*Position Number	Results Of Reference Check
I		III	
II		IV	

*See Page 3

Exhibit 1G

Preemployment Information

Dear Applicant:

In order for this college to comply with Equal Employment Opportunity and Affirmative Action regulations, we are required to compile summary data on the sex, ethnicity, handicapped status, and veteran status of all applicants. The information solicited on the reverse side of this letter is collected for the sole purpose of providing data to be used for statistical analysis; therefore, you should not identify yourself on this form. It should also be clearly understood that you have the option of supplying or not supplying the information requested.

This information, if provided, will neither enhance nor detract from your opportunity for employment at the college. Furthermore, information provided on this form will not become a part of any personnel file, nor will it be made available to those making employment decisions.

                                                        Director of Personnel

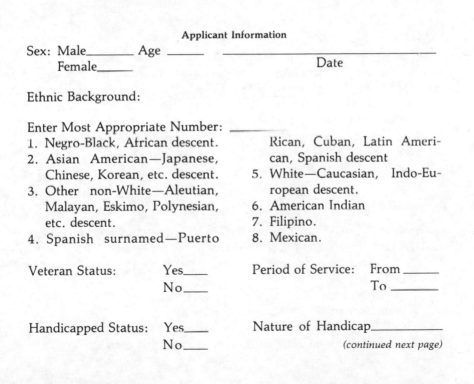

Applicant Information

Sex: Male_____ Age _____   _____
       Female_____   Date

Ethnic Background:

Enter Most Appropriate Number: _____
1. Negro-Black, African descent.   Rican, Cuban, Latin American, Spanish descent
2. Asian American—Japanese, Chinese, Korean, etc. descent.   5. White—Caucasian, Indo-European descent.
3. Other non-White—Aleutian, Malayan, Eskimo, Polynesian, etc. descent.   6. American Indian
                                          7. Filipino.
4. Spanish surnamed—Puerto   8. Mexican.

Veteran Status: Yes____   Period of Service: From _____
                     No____   To _____

Handicapped Status: Yes____   Nature of Handicap_____
                     No____   *(continued next page)*

(continued next page)

What Prompted You to Apply for Employment at the College?

1. Advertisement _____   Source _____
2. Announcement _____   Source _____
3. Advised to apply by: Faculty or Staff Member _____ Friend _____
                           Relative _____ Other _____
4. 24-hour Employment Opportunity Recording _____
5. Other _____

— —

For Personnel Office Use Only: Type of job
A. Executive, Administrative, Managerial   E. Technical and Paraprofessional
B. Faculty   F. Skilled craft
C. Professional nonfaculty   G. Service or Maintenance
D. Clerical or Secretarial

Exhibit 1H

How to Conduct an Employment Interview

The following article was prepared by Patricia Denton, of the University of Illinois—Chicago, for the "How-to" series published by the College and University Personnel Association.

Purpose

The objectives of a college or university employment interview are to learn about the applicant, determine the qualifications of the applicant, and describe to the applicant the institution and the employment it offers. Four major elements to consider in employment interviews are:
1. Skills of the interviewer.
2. Types of interviews.
3. Tools of interviewing.
4. Techniques of interviewing.

Interviewer Skills

An effective interviewer can be characterized by the possession of the qualities and expertise described below:
1. A combination of an objective viewpoint with an appreciation of human feelings.
2. Friendly attitude.
3. Pleasing personal appearance and manner.
4. Flexibility and freedom from strong preconceptions and biases.
5. Verbal precision in both expression and comprehension.

6. Professional experience in contacts with people of varying backgrounds and personal characteristics.
7. Training in interviewing techniques.
8. Full understanding of institutional structure, the types of work performed throughout, and the qualifications of employees required to implement work assignments.

Types of Interviews

Interviews may be categorized according to purpose, intensity, and coverage. Five categories in current use are:

1. *Preliminary interview.* A screening device used to determine whether a more extensive interview is worthwhile or necessary.

2. *Planned interview.* A training method for the new interviewer; it provides a definite plan of action to follow.

3. *Patterned interview.* A combination of direct and indirect questioning. The conversation is guided by the interviewer, but the applicant is encouraged to speak freely about relevant topics.

4. *Depth interview.* The most intensive method, which attempts to cover the complete history of the applicant. It includes questions about experience, education, and health as they relate to the job.

5. *Multiple judgment interview.* Requires several interviewers to see an applicant consecutively.

Tools of Interviewing

1. Employment application form.
2. Reference checks, test results, etc.
3. Position description of job vacancy and facts pertinent to departmental organization and physical arrangement.

Techniques of Interviewing

Prepare for the interview. Plan the interview (concerning objectives and timing) before seeing the applicant. Study the application, test results, reference checks (if attained in advance), job description, and other information. Provide for privacy. Rise to greet the applicant in welcome; call him or her by name; introduce yourself.

Outline the interview by objective. Point out that it is to the advantage of both applicant and institution to be sure that the right person is selected for the job. Explain that, by reviewing the job duties and the applicant's background, it can be determined whether the job is one in which he or she will be able to perform successfully. Explain the job in terms of its duties, future, hours, pay, special attractions, and undesirable features. *Don't oversell.* A candid, realistic approach encourages the applicant to discuss his or her goals, problems, and background. At this point, the applicant may either withdraw voluntarily or can be politely rejected.

Cover all background areas. The interview starts with the expected questions concerning work history and education. It is easy at this point to establish a friendly, informal, relaxed relationship. With rapport established, begin to probe the more personal aspects of the applicant's background.

Let the applicant do most of the talking. The cardinal rule of the interview is to let the applicant talk freely. Let the applicant volunteer maximum information. An interview in which the interviewer does more than *25 percent* of the talking is poorly conducted. Long silences can be a part of the interview, but not to an extent that the applicant becomes uncomfortable.

Take adequate time. An interview should not be hurried. Depending on the applicant's background and the position, a satisfactory interview may be completed in 30 minutes. Some may take longer.

Use a conversational manner. Phrase questions conversationally, but word them carefully to elicit below-the-surface facts; never accept loose generalizations. An adequate appraisal interview may include personal information about the applicant. However, any personal information elicited *must* be related to the job in question. It is important that *all* questions be relevant to the job.

Avoid leading questions. Leading questions are those that can be answered with a simple "yes" or "no." They give a clue to what is expected and provide the applicant with ready-made answers. Questions beginning with "Why," "Who," "When," "Where," or "How" encourage detailed, free-flowing answers. Never tell an applicant to hold information until a later and more appropriate point in the interview. Change the order of questions—not the applicant's order of response.

Avoid moral judgments. The interviewer's personal feelings must be kept hidden. The employment interview is not a counseling session, nor a place for criticism or admonition.

Record answers and dates. Make notes on the interview. It is not possible to remember every detail. Interview notes put information in an organized form which permits later objective analysis. Develop useful abbreviations. A gap of more than a month in the applicant's record and unaccounted-for periods of unemployment must be questioned.

Check inconsistencies carefully. When a contradiction in the date is found, call it to the applicant's attention in a friendly, noncritical manner. This will usually bring forth a correct answer. If the applicant isn't truthful, he or she becomes involved in further and more obvious contradictions.

Ordinarily, serious resistance to questions will not be encountered; if, however, the applicant does object to questions, there are two approaches to obtaining the necessary information while maintaining good will. The simplest method is to drop the question and return to it later when the applicant may have become less resistant. The second approach is more direct. Explain that these questions are asked of everyone to determine qualifications for the position. Such assurance as the following is then given: "But if you have some valid reason for withholding this information, naturally I won't insist." A pause after this statement often induces the applicant to speak up. The applicant is then in a position where he or she must provide the desired information or explain why he or she refuses to do so.

Create good will when concluding interview. If it is certain that the applicant is not qualified, conclude the interview at any logical stopping point. A simple explanation to the effect that no openings are available which fit the applicant's background, or that other applicants came nearer to meeting the overall job requirements, is generally all that is necessary. A "thank you for coming in" is always given.

If the applicant is qualified, however, he or she may be referred immediately or be asked to return for another appointment. Regardless of whether or not the applicant is hired, it is extremely important to retain good will by closing the interview graciously.

Exhibit 1I₁   **Written Reference Check**

┌   ┐

                [*address*]

└   ┘

Sir or Madam:

_____ has applied for a position with_____
_____. In order to assist us with the best possible placement of
this candidate, please fill out the form below and return it to us. We will
appreciate receiving your early reply in the enclosed self-addressed
envelope; information which you furnish will be kept in strict confidence.

_____ Personnel Specialist

- -

The candidate gave us the information below:
   Position: _____
   Supervisor:_____
   Period of employment: From_____ To _____
                        (month/year)   (month/year)

Is above information correct?   (   ) Yes   (   ) No

If no, please correct_____
_____

Were services satisfactory?   (   ) Yes   (   ) No
Would you reemploy?   (   ) Yes   (   ) No
Reason for leaving _____

	Excellent	Good	Fair	Poor
Character	( )	( )	( )	( )
Ability	( )	( )	( )	( )
Initiative	( )	( )	( )	( )
Reliability	( )	( )	( )	( )
Punctuality	( )	( )	( )	( )
Attendance	( )	( )	( )	( )
Popularity	( )	( )	( )	( )

Remarks:_____
        (Please use reverse side if necessary)

Signature:_____ Title: _____
Date: _____

Exhibit 1I$_2$

Written Reference Check

Date:

Re:

Dear Sir or Madam:

The above named applicant has applied to this college for a position as _____ and has given your name as a reference. The applicant states that he or she was employed by your firm from _____ to _____. We would appreciate your answering the following questions:

Position Held _____

Was termination voluntary? Yes_____ No_____. If no, explain _____

_____

_____

What is your assessment of this person in the following areas:

Skills_____

Attendance_____

Ability to work with others _____

All information furnished will be held in confidence. If you wish to make any additional comments about this applicant, please use the reverse side of this sheet.

Thank you very much for your cooperation.

Sincerely yours,

Personnel Administrator

Exhibit 1J₁

How to Conduct a Telephone, Preemployment Reference Check

This article was prepared by James M. Elliott and Ray T. Fortunato, of the Pennsylvania State University, for the "How-to" series published by the College and University Personnel Association.

Purpose

A preemployment reference check is intended to discover any undesirable factors in a job applicant's background prior to making an employment commitment.

The most desirable way to conduct such a check would be by personal visit. However, a telephone check is adequate and is less expensive. Letters or form letters rarely elicit information that is satisfactory. People hesitate to put in writing information they would give either in person or by telephone. Because of the stylized approach of the form letter, the necessary information might not be elicited. The telephone check can be guided into different avenues to gain information, depending on how the person giving the information is reacting to the questions being asked. This provides much more flexibility.

Preparation For the Telephone Call

1. The original interviewer should make the reference check. This person is probably the most familiar with the applicant and will have the background to do the necessary probing.

2. The telephone interviewer should make a check list of questions bearing on the particular applicant and the particular job he or she holds (or held) with the employer being interviewed.

3. Be sure to obtain permission from the applicant if there are plans to call a present employer. You cannot afford to jeopardize his or her present employment.

Conducting the Call

Call the person who had direct supervision over the applicant. Don't attempt to get the information secondhand, that is, from someone in a staff relationship (such as the personnel department) unless no other channel is available. The personnel office or accounting department can verify dates of employment and termination, but these employees are not usually in a position to give valuable information regarding the job applicant's former work habits, personal habits, performance, etc. Some "Dos" and "Don'ts" to consider are:

1. Don't leave a call-back if the individual you are trying to reach is not available. You may receive the return call when you're unable to discuss the applicant.

2. Identify yourself immediately, explain your position with your organization, and tell the party why you are calling about the applicant.

3. Assure your contact that any discussion you have will be held in confidence.

4. Ask if the individual is free to discuss the situation.

5. Try to establish rapport with the party you are calling. Information often can be exchanged more freely when the individual you are calling identifies with your organization, your position, or some other mutual point of interest.

6. Offer to have the party call back collect if you sense that the legitimacy of your call is doubted.

7. Give the party a thorough explanation of the position for which the applicant is being considered. The evaluation will be better if made in relation to a specific job.

8. Ask a general question such as "What is your opinion of how the applicant would fit into our vacancy?"

9. Let the person talk freely and answer without interruption. Often a question from you at the wrong time will shut off further information that could be beneficial.

10. Feel free to follow up and probe when you feel that the contact is reluctant to discuss certain factors. Many times, further explanation will elicit the information desired. A reference check benefits the applicant as much as a prospective employer; a placement in the wrong job could lead to ultimate unhappiness or even dismissal.

11. Be alert for obvious pauses in answering questions. Often these are a sign that further questions may bring additional information that might not otherwise have been received.

12. Don't be concerned with time needed for the conversation. A few dollars for a toll call could save untold amounts in expense in making the wrong hire.

13. Don't hang up until you're sure that you know the opinion of the person called. Frequently, you will receive ambiguous answers. The person called may give very little useful information. A technique that frequently works is to summarize the conversation by making either of the following two statements:

    a. "I take it that you don't recommend the applicant very highly for the position," or

   b. "I take it that you recommend the applicant very highly for the
      position."

   14. Check your list of questions to be sure everything has been
covered.

   15. Always close the call by asking the party with whom you are talking, "Would you reemploy the applicant?" Often this question brings
forth information that you were unable to get by other questions.

   16. Be sure to thank the contact for his or her help.

Suggested Questions for the Call

   After providing background information to the telephone contact on
the vacancy to be filled, ask a general response question (such as No. 8 in
the list above), then go to more specific questions, for example:

   1. How did the applicant get along with others with whom he or she
      worked?
   2. How did the applicant get along with supervisors?
   3. Did the applicant have any personal habits that you consider to be
      negative?
   4. How was the applicant's health?
   5. Did you consider the applicant to be reliable?
   6. Did the applicant meet commitments?
   7. Why did the applicant leave your company?
   8. Did the applicant pay his or her bills?
   9. Do you know of any criminal record?
   10. What was the nature of the applicant's work with you?
   11. Has the applicant been bypassed on promotions with your com-
       pany?
   12. Would you reemploy the applicant?
   13. What are applicant's strengths? Weaknesses?
   14. Is there anything else you'd like to tell me about the applicant?

Exhibit 1J$_2$

TELEPHONE REFERENCE QUESTIONAIRE

| 1. | CANDIDATE'S NAME |
| 2. | POSITION APPLIED FOR |

3. NAME AND TITLE OF RESPONDENT

4. RESPONDENT'S COMPANY OR FIRM

"The above named Candidate has stated that he/she was

employed as a 5._____

from 6._____ to 7._____ by your company

8. "Can you confirm ?" ☐ yes ☐ no

9. "What were some of his/her responsibilities ?"

10. "How would you rate this person ?"

Quality of work ☐	*Learning ability* ☐	RATE AS: ABOVE AVERAGE (AA)
Quantity of work ☐	*Congenialty* ☐	AVERAGE (A)
Attitude ☐	*Attendance* ☐	BELOW AVERAGE (BA)

11. *Strong points*

12. *Weak points*

13. *"Would you rehire?"* ☐ yes ☐ no

GENERAL OBSERVATIONS

| SIGNATURE | DATE |
| | |

Exhibit 1K$_1$

Personnel Referral	Office of Personnel Services An Equal Opportunity Employer		Date	

<table>
<tr><td rowspan="9">TO</td><td colspan="2">Departmental Representative</td><td>Requisition Date</td><td>Requisition Number</td></tr>
<tr><td colspan="2">Department and Telephone</td><td colspan="2">Position</td></tr>
<tr><td colspan="2">Address</td><td colspan="2"></td></tr>
<tr><td colspan="2" rowspan="6">_____is being referred to you as a candidate for the requisitioned position specified* on this referral at the rate indicated.** All employment offers will be made by the Employment Office.</td><td rowspan="6">SKILL TESTS</td><td>Typing
w.p.m.</td></tr>
<tr><td>Accuracy
%</td></tr>
<tr><td>Shorthand
w.p.m.</td></tr>
<tr><td>Spelling</td></tr>
</table>

	FROM:	PERSONNEL SERVICES	Candidate is a ☐ former ☐ current college employee

<table>
<tr><td rowspan="5">COMMENTS</td><td rowspan="5"></td><td rowspan="5">WORK-STUDY INFORMATION</td><td>Department</td></tr>
<tr><td>Maximum work-study earnings for the school year are:</td></tr>
<tr><td></td></tr>
<tr><td>S</td></tr>
<tr><td>☐ Summer   ☐ Fall   ☐ Spring</td></tr>
</table>

TO EMPLOYING DEPARTMENT:

1. WHEN HIRING DECISION IS MADE, PLEASE ADVISE PERSONNEL SERVICES IMMEDIATELY.

2. This form must be completed, signed by departmental representative, and returned to Personnel Services once a hiring decision has been made.

3. IF APPLICANT IS ACCEPTED, complete section 1 below, sign, date and return two yellow copies to Personnel Services as an attachment to the appointment form of the individual hired.

4. IF APPLICANT IS REJECTED, complete section 2 below, sign, date and return two yellow copies to Personnel Services.

5. ACCEPTED CANDIDATE MUST complete preemployment papers in the Payroll Office before this appointment can become effective.

---

1. ☐ Applicant is accepted and will report to work on   at a salary of $
   ☐ per hour   ☐ per month   ☐ per year

2. ☐ Applicant is rejected.
   Please definitively explain your reason for rejection in terms of the specific strengths and weaknesses of the candidate.

Beyond the usual coordination with Personnel Services (i.e., listing staff vacancies, etc.) did you exercise other affirmative action recruitment efforts in an attempt to have minorities or females apply?	☐ Yes ☐ No	IF YES, PLEASE EXPLAIN ON THE REVERSE SIDE

MY SIGNATURE ON THIS FORM SIGNIFIES THAT THE APPROPRIATE COLLEGE PROCEDURES RELATIVE TO EEO HAVE TAKEN PLACE

Date of Interview	Date of Action Taken	Signature of Employing Department Representative

Return To Personnel Services

Exhibit 1K₂ **Applicant Referral Form**

Date: _____ Applicant's Name _____

TO: _____ Position Applied For: _____

FROM: _____   _____

I have referred the above-named applicant and the attached employment papers to you for your evaluation. Please check the appropriate response below and where applicable, please add your comments.

Your comments are useful in determining the extent to which we have been able to assist you in reviewing applicants. Please write your comments below while the interview is still fresh in your mind.

This form and application should be returned to us shortly after your interview. Upon request, all applicant referral forms will be made available to you to help in your final selection.

Please advise the applicant to return to Personnel Services after the interview.

1. (   ) I wish to hire this candidate. Please call me to discuss starting date and salary.

2. (   ) I *may* want to hire this candidate. Please refer others before I make a decision. **My Comments Are Written Below.**

3. (   ) This candidate is *not* suitable for this job. **My Comments Are Written Below.**

_____

_____

(add lines as necessary)

_____

(Signature of Department Inverviewer)   (Date)

. . . . (**For Personnel Office Use Only**) . . . .

_____

(Employment Source)

( )S   ( )R   ( )E   ( )VV   ( )EO   ( )H   ( )Y

Exhibit 1L$_1$

Letters to Job Applicants
Who Were *Not* Selected

Thank you for your application for employment. Unfortunately, your application reached us after the position you applied for had been closed. We do not have a job vacancy at this time that would utilize your educational and work background. However, we will retain your application in our active file for one year.

Sincerely yours,

Personnel Administrator

Exhibit 1L$_2$

Thank you for your application for employment. Unfortunately, at this time we do not have a position vacancy that would utilize your educational and work background.

We will retain your application in our active file for one year. We appreciate your interest in _____ College and wish you success in obtaining a position.

Sincerely yours,

Personnel Administrator

Exhibit 1L$_3$

We have received your application for employment opportunities with _____ College.

This position was filled by an in-house applicant and in no way reflects upon your qualifications or abilities.

Your application will be retained in our active file for one year. We appreciate your interest in _____ College and wish you success in obtaining a position.

Sincerely yours,

Personnel Administrator

Exhibit 1L₄

We have received your application for employment opportunities with _____
College.

After careful review of the applications submitted, we have scheduled interviews only for
those individuals whose education and experience most closely relates to the requirements
of the position.

Your application will be retained in our active file for one year. We appreciate your interest
in _____ College and wish you success in obtaining a position.

Sincerely yours,

Personnel Administrator

Exhibit 1L₅

It was a pleasure meeting with you recently to discuss employment opportunities at _____
College.

We have interviewed many fine applicants for this position and the employment background and qualifications of each applicant have been carefully reviewed.

At this time we feel that another candidate has specific work experience and an educational
background that are more closely related to the duties of this position. However, we will retain your application and contact you should an opening commensurate with your qualifications become available.

Thank you for giving us the opportunity to meet with you to discuss your qualifications.

Sincerely yours,

Personnel Administrator

Exhibit 1M$_1$

<table>
<tr><td colspan="4" align="center">Change of Status</td></tr>
<tr><td>Supportive Operating Staff Personnel</td><td colspan="2"></td><td align="right">CONFIDENTIAL</td></tr>
</table>

Name (As Signed For Check Signature)	Department		Employee Number
	Effective Date		Account Number

Check Action Desired and Complete Section Indicated	☐ Hire 1, 2, 3 ☐ Classification Change 4, 2 ☐ Transfer-Promotion 4, 2		☐ Termination or Separation 5, 6 ☐ Rate Change 2
1. Hire	New Employee ☐ Rehire ☐ Return to Work ☐ Reinstated ☐		Job Title _____ Classification Grade _____ Hours Per Work Week _____ FLSA Exempt ☐ Nonexempt ☐

2. Rate Change	Probationary ☐ Merit ☐ Promotion ☐ Annual Review ☐ Other ☐			Old Rate	New Rate
			Hourly	_____	_____
			Biweekly	_____	_____
			Monthly	_____	_____
			Annual	_____	_____

3. Fringe Benefits	Eligible for: Group Life Insurance ☐ Medical Insurance ☐	Total Disability Program ☐ Retirement Program ☐

4. Transfer or Promotion	Employee Request ☐ University Transfer ☐ New Position ☐ Other ☐	Department Job Title Classification Grade	From _____ _____ _____	To _____ _____ _____

5. Leave of Absence	Medical ☐ With full pay ☐ Without pay ☐ Other ☐ With part pay ☐ Leave Period from _____ through_____ Leave extended _____ days through _____ Reason for leave _____ <center>(Attach doctor's statement if sick leave)</center>

6. Termination	Retired ☐ Voluntary Resignation ☐ Layoff ☐	Military ☐ Discharged ☐ Deceased ☐

7. Miscellaneous	Last Day Worked _____ Pay through _____ Reason for Termination _____ Eligible for Reemployment Yes ☐ No ☐	Exit interview-Yes No Days Vacation Pay_____ Days Sick Leave _____

8. Remarks	

Approval	Department Head	Date	Business Manager	Date

Distribution: 1. Payroll   3. Personnel File
2. Department Head/Director   4. Employee

Exhibit 1M₂

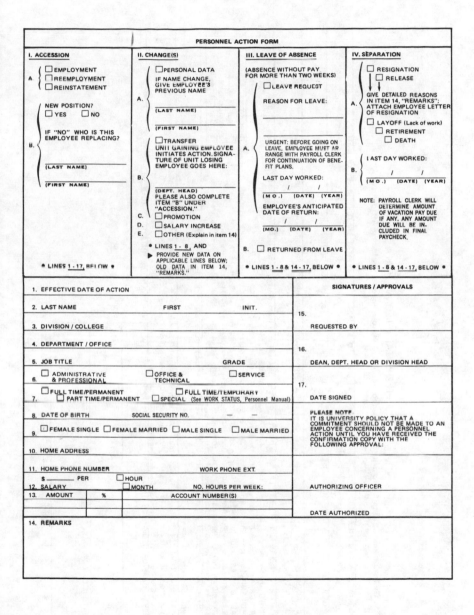

PERSONNEL ACTION FORM			
I. ACCESSION	**II. CHANGE(S)**	**III. LEAVE OF ABSENCE**	**IV. SEPARATION**

I. ACCESSION

A. ☐ EMPLOYMENT ☐ REEMPLOYMENT ☐ REINSTATEMENT

NEW POSITION? ☐ YES ☐ NO

IF "NO" WHO IS THIS EMPLOYEE REPLACING?

B. (LAST NAME) _____

(FIRST NAME) _____

● LINES 1 - 17, BELOW ●

II. CHANGE(S)

A. ☐ PERSONAL DATA
IF NAME CHANGE, GIVE EMPLOYEE'S PREVIOUS NAME

(LAST NAME)

(FIRST NAME)

☐ TRANSFER
UNIT GAINING EMPLOYEE INITIATES ACTION. SIGNATURE OF UNIT LOSING EMPLOYEE GOES HERE:

B. (DEPT. HEAD)
PLEASE ALSO COMPLETE ITEM "B" UNDER "ACCESSION."

C. ☐ PROMOTION
D. ☐ SALARY INCREASE
E. ☐ OTHER (Explain in item 14)

● LINES 1 - 8, AND
▶ PROVIDE NEW DATA ON APPLICABLE LINES BELOW; OLD DATA IN ITEM 14, "REMARKS."

III. LEAVE OF ABSENCE

(ABSENCE WITHOUT PAY FOR MORE THAN TWO WEEKS)

☐ LEAVE REQUEST

REASON FOR LEAVE:
_____
_____

A. URGENT: BEFORE GOING ON LEAVE, EMPLOYEE MUST ARRANGE WITH PAYROLL CLERK FOR CONTINUATION OF BENEFIT PLANS.

LAST DAY WORKED:
/ /
(M O.) (DATE) (YEAR)

EMPLOYEE'S ANTICIPATED DATE OF RETURN:
/ /
(MO.) (DATE) (YEAR)

B. ☐ RETURNED FROM LEAVE

● LINES 1 - 8 & 14 - 17, BELOW ●

IV. SEPARATION

☐ RESIGNATION
☐ RELEASE

A. GIVE DETAILED REASONS IN ITEM 14, "REMARKS"; ATTACH EMPLOYEE LETTER OF RESIGNATION

☐ LAYOFF (Lack of work)
☐ RETIREMENT
☐ DEATH

LAST DAY WORKED:

B. / /
(MO.) (DATE) (YEAR)

NOTE: PAYROLL CLERK WILL DETERMINE AMOUNT OF VACATION PAY DUE IF ANY. ANY AMOUNT DUE WILL BE INCLUDED IN FINAL PAYCHECK.

● LINES 1 - 8 & 14 - 17, BELOW ●

---

1. EFFECTIVE DATE OF ACTION

2. LAST NAME   FIRST   INIT.

3. DIVISION / COLLEGE

4. DEPARTMENT / OFFICE

5. JOB TITLE   GRADE

6. ☐ ADMINISTRATIVE & PROFESSIONAL   ☐ OFFICE & TECHNICAL   ☐ SERVICE

7. ☐ FULL TIME/PERMANENT   ☐ FULL TIME/TEMPORARY
☐ PART TIME/PERMANENT   ☐ SPECIAL (See WORK STATUS, Personnel Manual)

8. DATE OF BIRTH   SOCIAL SECURITY NO.   — —

9. ☐ FEMALE SINGLE   ☐ FEMALE MARRIED   ☐ MALE SINGLE   ☐ MALE MARRIED

10. HOME ADDRESS

11. HOME PHONE NUMBER   WORK PHONE EXT

$ _____ PER   ☐ HOUR
12. SALARY   ☐ MONTH   NO. HOURS PER WEEK:

13. AMOUNT   %   ACCOUNT NUMBER(S)

14. REMARKS

SIGNATURES / APPROVALS

15. REQUESTED BY

16. DEAN, DEPT. HEAD OR DIVISION HEAD

17. DATE SIGNED

PLEASE NOTE:
IT IS UNIVERSITY POLICY THAT A COMMITMENT SHOULD NOT BE MADE TO AN EMPLOYEE CONCERNING A PERSONNEL ACTION UNTIL YOU HAVE RECEIVED THE CONFIRMATION COPY WITH THE FOLLOWING APPROVAL:

AUTHORIZING OFFICER

DATE AUTHORIZED

(Note: This form should be prepared in quadruplicate.)

Exhibit 1N

SUPPLEMENTAL PERSONNEL DATA

NOTE: This supplemental staff information is required to prepare various reports (including Affirmative Action) and to serve Staff Benefits, emergency and public information needs of the University.

NAME (LAST, FIRST, MIDDLE)	SOCIAL SECURITY NUMBER	MARITAL STATUS	PLACE OF BIRTH

DATE OF BIRTH	NAME OF SPOUSE (LAST, FIRST, MIDDLE)	SPOUSE'S OCCUPATION	

LOCAL ADDRESS	LOCAL PHONE NO.	CAMPUS ADDRESS (ROOM, BLDG.)	CAMPUS PHONE NO.

CHECK THE GROUP IN WHICH YOU CLASSIFY YOURSELF: (This information is needed for University Affirmative Action Program.)

1 WHITE (Non-Hispanic, Origins of Europe, North Africa, or Middle East.)

2 BLACK (Non-Hispanic, Origins in any of the Black Racial Groups of Africa.)

3 HISPANIC (Mexican, Puerto Rican, Cuban, Cent. or So. American or other Spanish Cultural origins, regardless of race.)

4 ASIAN OR PACIFIC ISLANDER (Origins in any of original peoples of the Far East, Southeast Asia, the Indian Sub-continent, or the Pacific Islands. Includes China, Japan, Korea, Philippine Islands and Samoa.)

5 AMERICAN INDIAN OR ALASKAN NATIVE (Origins in any of original peoples of No. America and who maintain cultural identification through tribal affiliation or community recognition.)

SEX: ☐ MALE ☐ FEMALE

CHECK ONE:
1 Native U.S.A.
2 Naturalized
3 Non-Citizen U.S.A.

DO YOU HAVE A PHYSICAL OR MENTAL DISABILITY AFFECTING YOUR EMPLOYMENT? (If YES, SPECIFY)

☐ YES ☐ NO

EDUCATIONAL LEVEL 1 Grammer School Credit 2 Grammer School Graduate 3 High School Credit 4 High School Graduate or G.E.D.
5 Vocational or Business School Credit 6 Vocational or Business School Graduate 7 College or University Credit
COLLEGE GRADUATE: 8 Bachelor's 9 Master's 10 Doctor's

NOTIFY IN CASE OF EMERGENCY (NAME)	TELEPHONE NO.	NAMES AND BIRTHDATES OF CHILDREN

ADDRESS		

SIGNATURE OF EMPLOYEE	DATE	

Exhibit 1"O"

POSITION VACANCY ANNOUNCEMENT

JOB CLASSIFICATION:

DEPARTMENT
SUPERVISOR
DUTIES

QUALIFICATIONS

EXPERIENCE

NEW POSITION ◯   REPLACEMENT ◯
POSITION FUNDED BY   ◯   GRANT FUNDS ◯
RANGE

POSTING DATE

an equal opportunity/affirmative action employer

Exhibit 1P

Date:_____

Social Security Number:_____

Check One:

____Service Staff

____Office Staff

____Managerial   **Resignation Form**

____Technical

I, _____, wish to resign from

                          Name

my job, classified as _____, at

                                    Title

this college for one of the following reasons: (Please check one)

____To Accept Other Employment   ____Pregnancy

____To Be Married   ____Return to School

____Illness   ____Family Reasons

____Personal Reasons   ____Leaving the Area

____To Enter Self-Employment   ____Working Conditions

____Military Service

Other_____

_____

My last day of actual work is_____

                                    Date

Name _____

            Signature

Home   Address_____

_____

— —

FOR OFFICE USE ONLY

Received by_____   ____I.D. Attached

                                        ____Insurance Explained

Exhibit 1Q₁

*(Note that this exhibit is in two parts: in the first section, actual questions for the inter-
viewer to use are indicated. This is direct guidance for the line of conversation. The second
section evokes retrospective analysis on the part of the interviewer to gauge the results and
further implications of the interview.)*

Exit Interview

I understand that you are leaving. Before you do, we would like to
discuss your experience with this college.

1. Do you have another job? _____ If yes, Where?_____
   What is new rate of pay? _____
2. What kind of work have you been doing here? _____
3. What kind of work do you like best?_____ Why? _____
4. When you started here, were you introduced to the people you
   worked with? _____
5. Were you fully trained for your job? _____ By whom? _____
6. How did you and your supervisor get along? _____
7. What was good about your relationship? _____
8. What, if anything, was not so good? _____
9. How do you feel about your pay? _____
10. How do you feel about your progress at the college?_____
11. What have you liked best about your job here? _____
12. What have you disliked about your job here? _____
13. Why are you leaving? _____
14. Why at this particular time? _____
15. Would you want to stay if it were possible to work out some
    changes? _____ What changes? _____
Interviewer's evaluation of real reasons for termination: _____
_____
_____

Interviewer _____

Date of Interview_____

Reviewed by _____
                      Supervisor of Employment

(Note: Use reverse side of this form for "Termination evaluation.")

Termination Evaluation

Date_____19____

Name _____ Supervisor_____ Department_____

Job_____ Dates of
Employment _____to_____

(The points listed below are intended as a guide to the termination interviewer to help in interpreting information recorded on the reverse side of
this form. This is not meant to be a conclusive analysis of data.)

1. How does wage rate at employee's new job compare with our rate?
2. Was he or she hired for this particular work?
3. Is there evidence of poor selection?
4. Was there proper job orientation?
5. Was there adequate training?
6. Did employee have good supervision?
7. Did employee have enough supervision?
8. Does the employee have a reasonable attitude?
9. Has employee been overlooked?
10. Were college policies made clear to this employee?
11. Does he or she have legitimate complaints?
12. Does the employee have a healthy attitude?
13. Is the reason indicated the real reason for termination? Can termina-
    tion be avoided?
14. What is the full story?
15. Are the employee's ideas for changes reasonable?

Final disposition: Quit_____ Maternity_____
                    Involuntary (Illness, family problems, etc.) _____
                    Discharge _____

*Selection Rating (Circle one):   1   2   3   4

*Rating for Rehire (Circle one):   1   2   3   4

        Check original evaluation of employment interview.

*1. Outstanding   2. Well Qualified   3. Marginally Qualified   4. Unsatisfactory

Exhibit 1Q$_2$

(Note that in this exhibit, the questions simply record the information obtained by the interview and provide indirect guidance for the interviewer. The post-interview analysis is as important as the orderly procedure of the interview.)

Exit Interview

A. The Job Itself
1. Did employee feel he or she was under- or over-qualified for the job, based on training and experience?
Underqualified____ Overqualified____ Neither____
2. Did employee perceive this job as important? Yes____ No____
3. Did job meet expectations and aspirations of employee? Yes____ No____
4. Did employee feel a sense of progress in the job? Yes____ No____
5. Did employee feel he or she had sufficient freedom on the job? Yes____ No____
6. Did employee like the work environment (hours, space, equipment, etc.)? Yes____ No____
7. Did employee feel that there was opportunity for advancement? Yes____ No____
8. Did employee feel secure in the job? Yes____ No____

Comments_____

B. Wage and Salary Fringes
1. Did employee feel that there was adequate orientation for the job? Yes____ No____
2. Did employee feel salary was adequate for work performed? Yes____ No____
3. Did employee feel that salary was competitive for comparable job? Yes____ No____
4. Did employee feel fringe benefits were adequate? Yes____ No____
Suggested improvements _____
5. Did employee feel that vacation allowances were fair? Yes____ No____
6. Did employee feel that sick leave allowances were fair? Yes____ No____

Comments_____

C. Relationship with Supervisor
1. Did employee feel that supervisor was fair and consistent in use of authority? Yes____ No____

2. Did employee feel that there were adequate lines of communication with supervisor? Yes____ No____
3. Did employee have any participation in decision making? Yes____ No____
4. Did employee feel that supervisor gave adequate assistance and training? Yes____ No____
5. Did employee feel that supervisor took an interest in his or her welfare and progress? Yes____ No____

Comments_____

_____

D. Relationship with Work Group
   1. Did employee enjoy working with coworkers? Yes____ No____
E. Relationship with Organization
   Employee's rating of the college, on a 1–10 scale (1 is best rating):
      1   2   3   4   5   6   7   8   9   10
What was employee's general attitude?_____
Interviewer's comments_____

_____

_____

2. compensation

A sound wage and salary administration program is essential to the success of any enterprise, including a college or university. Yet, many colleges have failed to develop formal wage and salary programs; instead, they use informal, paternalistic approaches, which treat each employee individually. Equal pay requirements, external competition, and internal equity considerations make informal approaches increasingly unworkable.

A formal wage and salary program is characterized by uniform, written standards that guide individual pay decisions. Such standards should not be viewed as substitutes for human judgment, but rather as aids to consistent and objective pay administration. Administrators should strive to develop a pay plan that provides for a reasonable balance between rigidity and flexibility. The ideal pay plan should be viewed as a means to an end and not as an end in itself.

Administrators should not initiate a wage and salary program without sufficient staff or consultant help; the best intentions do not substitute for expert knowledge. Consultant resources that small colleges frequently overlook are wage and salary managers and personnel directors from large institutions.

Objectives of a Wage and Salary Program

A comprehensive wage and salary program is a principal factor in attracting, retaining, and rewarding employees. This is crucial to colleges, since they are labor-intensive operations. The following list, while not exhaustive, includes the major objectives of a comprehensive compensation program:

1. To insure that college compensation policies are consistent with applicable laws and regulations, such as equal pay and affirmative action.

2. To keep the institution competitive with other employers and aid in attracting and retaining competent employees.

3. To provide internal equity, which bases pay potential on a measurement of the duties and responsibilities of jobs.

4. To provide incentive and rewards for good performance.

5. To foster unity and simplicity of operation so that the pay plan is easy to implement, maintain, and understand, and can be fully communicated to employees.

6. To give administrators an objective basis on which to make compensation decisions.

7. To accommodate timely and equitable wage adjustments for increased job responsibility.

When colleges approach wage and salary administration on an ad hoc basis, they risk grave financial penalties and serious employee morale problems. Sound plans can be implemented and maintained with a minimum of cost and staff commitment.

Support For Pay Plan

It is essential that senior college officers, including the governing board, support the compensation plan and its administrators. Exceptions to established policy and practices can destroy the employees' confidence in the plan and thus nullify its value. Accordingly, pay decisions should be based on reasonable pay plan factors, not on political considerations. Consistent administration is the key to employee acceptance.

Responsibility For Compensation Administration

The assignment of responsibility for compensation administration is important to any organization. Authority to administer the pay plan ideally should be vested in the person or department responsible for personnel services. This does not preclude review from higher levels, nor should it prohibit participation by deans, directors, and other managers in determining specific pay rates for employees under their supervision. In fact, the ideal plan should *require* participation by line administrators concerning performance appraisal and pay rate determination, although not in decisions relative to pay levels (pay grades or classification levels).

Reason For a Formalized Program

Poor employee morale can seriously hamper an organization, and inconsistent, unfair pay practices contribute to poor morale more directly than any other single factor. Conversely, a formalized, equitable pay plan can do more than any other program to maintain positive, harmonious employee relations.

A new employee is generally satisfied with the rate of pay on being hired and usually remains so unless he or she learns that others doing comparable work are earning more. If this occurs, dissatisfaction will affect morale and productivity and will soon spread to other employees. Such discontent invites union organization activities.

Jobs To Be Included in the Pay Plan

The initial step in devising a compensation plan is to determine which jobs it will include. Many colleges have separate pay plans for (1) clerical, (2) food service, and (3) maintenance employees, and still another plan for (4) supervisory and administrative employees. The first three groups are generally *nonexempt* from overtime and the fourth is usually *exempt* from overtime. The nonexempt groups typically include unskilled, semi-skilled, and skilled personnel (those in crafts and trades, and technicians). A separate plan for the fourth group, all supervisory employees, helps to impress on them—particularly first-line administrators—that they are integral members of the management team.

Public Policy Considerations

Public policy on compensation is expressed in federal and state laws and regulations. The Fair Labor Standards Act (FLSA), more commonly referred to as the "Wage and Hour Law," articulates a national compensation policy through its provisions for minimum wages and overtime compensation. Additional national policy is expressed in the Equal Pay Act, which requires "equal pay for equal work." Various state laws promulgate other regulations covering minimum wages, overtime requirements, and equal pay standards. Employers should be conversant with the provisions of these laws and with their applicability to colleges and universities.

In 1976, the United States Supreme Court, in the *Usery* v. *League of Cities* case, ruled that the minimum wage and overtime provisions of FLSA are not applicable to *public* colleges and universities.[3] However, the Court appeared to retain the applicability of the Equal Pay Act. The statute in its entirety remains applicable to independent institutions of higher education. Summary analysis of the Wage and Hour Law and the Equal Pay Act are contained in NACUBO's *Federal Regulations and the Employment Practices of Colleges and Universities.*

Job Analysis

An early step in building a compensation program is *job analysis*, the collection of information concerning duties, responsibilities, organiza-

---

[3]National League of Cities v. Usery, 426 U.S. 833 (1976).

tional relationships, and educational and experiential requirements of jobs. Knowledge of this information is prerequisite to determining the relative value of a job.

Methods of Job Analysis

Job facts are usually gathered by questionnaire and interview. Since there are advantages and disadvantages to both, a combination of the two usually produces the most valid results. The shortcomings of a questionnaire include a wide variation of responses, inability of some employees to express themselves in writing, and the possible resentment of employees when requested to complete forms. A major advantage of the questionnaire is that information can be obtained from several employees within a short time. Further, the employee is more likely to accept the results of subsequent job evaluation if he or she supplied the facts about the job.

An interview has the advantage of affording personal contact and observation of the employee in the work setting. Whether the questionnaire, interview, or a combination approach is used, information solicited should include a description of what the employee does, how it is done, why it is done, degree of independence of action by the employee, and the skill required to do the work. (See Exhibits $2A_1$ and $2A_2$.)

Position Descriptions

Once the job analysis is complete, the information must be summarized in a form commonly referred to as a "position description" or "job description." The position description provides a standardized format for the job information, which is also useful later in the job evaluation process. (See Exhibits $2B_1$ and $2B_2$.)

Position descriptions should be clear and concise, and they should be carefully reviewed for accuracy and for appropriate and consistent use of terminology, that is, the terms used to describe work activities. Next, management should determine that the work assigned is necessary and that essential tasks are grouped in the most efficient manner. The position description can also assist the manager in explaining to new employees the performance standards expected of them.

Position descriptions should be prepared by employees and checked by their supervisors. This procedure will reduce misunderstandings concerning work assignments and performance standards; it also contributes to the accuracy of position descriptions. The position description is to be distinguished from a statement on how well the incumbent employee performs the job; the information in the position description should relate *only* to the job itself, *not* to the person who currently holds the job.

The formats for position descriptions are numerous; there does not appear to be one in particular that has evolved as the usually accepted standard. However, these descriptions have common elements, such as (1) job or position title; (2) a brief summary of job function; (3) a listing of job duties typically required or performed; (4) percentage of time for each duty required or performed, using a common basis of monthly, weekly, or daily; (5) occasional duties; (6) minimum qualifications, such as education, experience, skills, licenses, or certifications; (7) additional preferred qualifications; (8) explanation of organizational lines and the supervision that is exercised or received; (9) signature of employee; (10) signature of supervisor; and (11) date. Some formats are designed to elicit additional information, but the elements listed above provide the basis for developing a comprehensive position description library.

Job Analysis-Position Description Shortcut

The two chronological phases of gathering job facts described above (job analysis and position description) constitute the "textbook approach" to performing this task. The textbook approach certainly provides full, detailed information, but is so exhaustive that it may require considerable time and staff. Small colleges can employ a shortcut and still obtain valid job information. This shortcut, in effect, consolidates the two phases. Under the textbook approach, if the questionnaire method is used, someone from the business or personnel office or an outside consultant must design the questionnaire, review the completed forms, and write the condensed position description from the information provided.

Using the shortcut, a format for a position description is prepared. The employee and supervisor use this form to describe the employee's job duties and responsibilities under major headings, including the approximate percentage of time each major function or activity requires. The completed descriptions should then be reviewed for clarity and completeness by the person responsible for administration of the compensation plan. Descriptions may be summarized to insure uniformity of terms and key factors preparatory to initiation of the job evaluation process.

Job Evaluation

Following the collection of job information and the preparation of a position description, job evaluation can begin. This is essentially a systematic method or procedure for determining the fair value of a particular job and its difficulty (complexity or importance) in relation to other jobs. The process measures job duties against a predetermined yardstick and assesses job worth; it has nothing to do with an employee's performance, ability, potential, attitude, or quantity or quality of work. Job evaluation is entirely different from employee evaluation, which is described in Chapter 4.

Four traditional job evaluation methods are in use today: (1) ranking, (2) classification, (3) point, and (4) factor comparison. Each has its advantages and disadvantages and each varies in the time required for evaluation and in the preciseness of the evaluation. In recent years a new approach has evolved called the "market method."

Ranking Method

The ranking method of job evaluation compares one job to another in order to determine which is most difficult or important. A distinguishing characteristic of this method is that comparison is frequently on the basis of an entire job, that is, the job is *not* segmented or broken down into job characteristics, factors, or points for purposes of measurement. In the last few years, job factors have been used in the ranking method to improve its accuracy. In order to differentiate between jobs, the evaluator must learn the inherent and subtle differences in jobs through a careful review of each job description or job analysis questionnaire.

After the evaluator(s) has become versed in the jobs to be ranked, the job or allocation factor(s) must be selected. The allocation factors are simply criteria that assist the evaluator in ranking. If only one factor is used, it is generally "job difficulty," that is, which job is more difficult to perform or is more important. Generally, more than one allocation factor is used in order to achieve a more accurate ranking. Factors may include physical effort required, levels of supervision required, personal contacts, and others. Using these allocation factors, comparisons are made between jobs in order to provide a hierarchy.

After the jobs have been ranked, the rankings are converted into dollar values, which are explained in the section "Pay Structure and Pricing" later in this chapter. The ranking method is based on the premise that jobs differ from each other and that pay levels and pay potential can be determined by ranking them in order of difficulty or importance.

Following is a step-by-step summary of the ranking method:

1. Arrange all jobs by title in order of their increasing value to the institution.

    A. Collect information about each job.

    B. Study individual position descriptions.

C. Rank the jobs, based on (A) and (B) above, regarding such factors as:

   (1) Responsibility for items of value or for consequences of performance.
   (2) Education, skills, and training required.
   (3) Experience required.
   (4) Level of supervision required.
   (5) Level of supervision given others.
   (6) Working conditions.

2. Establish a pay rate for each job title around which individual rates for the job should cluster. While there should be room for exception, it is best to discourage wide variations from the clustering effect. If wide variations occur, consider a different placement in the ranking hierarchy.

3. Rates of pay should reflect judgments of relative worth to the institution as well as awareness of competitive rates in the labor market from which employees are hired.

An example of a partial table of pay rates follows:

Rank	Job Title	Hourly Rate
1	Electrician, Plumber	$5.25
2	Stationary Engineer	
	Maintenance Worker	4.75
3	Guard	4.50
4	Custodian, Groundsworker	4.00
5	Cook	3.75
6	Food Service Worker	3.25

The ranking method of job evaluation is easily understood, requires limited expertise, and is inexpensive, since it can be accomplished in a short period with limited staff. Unfortunately, the simplicity of the approach is also its greatest shortcoming. An evaluator may judge job difficulty or importance on the basis of one dominant job characteristic, to the exclusion of other characteristics. The ranking method may not have the confidence of the employees, since it is considered the most subjective of the job evaluation methods. Another disadvantage of the ranking approach is that it can determine only that one job is more difficult than another; it can not indicate *how much* more difficult or important one job is than another.

Techniques devised to remedy some of these weaknesses, by quantifying the ranking approach, can transform several of the subjective disadvantages into objective advantages. The ranking method is practical for small institutions that have a limited number of jobs and limited staff to administer the compensation plan.

Classification Method

The classification method requires development of a number of grades or classes of jobs that reflect overall job difficulty or importance, and against which each job is measured. The federal Civil Service Commission's job grade system is an example of the classification method. In this method, an evaluator compares each position description with the classification standard and slots the job into the classification level or grade that best describes its characteristics and difficulty.

The most problematic element of the classification method is writing the classification level or grade description, sometimes referred to as the classification standard or specification. The compensable factors for determining job difficulty must be reflected in the classification level description. These factors typically include job knowledge required, judgment exercised, analysis or decision making required, and education and experience needed to perform the job. The classification method is easily understood and it is possible for smaller institutions to employ a consultant to write the level or grade descriptions and then for a small committee of college officers to assign jobs to the appropriate grade. The classification method is an efficient approach to job evaluation for small colleges. (See Exhibits $2C_1$ and $2C_2$.)

Following is a step-by-step summary of the classification method:

1. Collect information about each job.
    A. Study position descriptions so that those describing similar jobs can be grouped together.

    B. Analyze the descriptions to identify similarities, based on such factors as the following:
       (1) Responsibility for items of value or for consequences of performance.
       (2) Education, skills, or training required.
       (3) Experience required.
       (4) Judgment exercised.
       (5) Level of supervision required.
       (6) Level of supervision given others.
       (7) Working conditions.

2. Write class specifications for each grouping of position descriptions sharing similar characteristics.

3. Survey jobs in the local labor market for each classification, using the class specifications as the basic tool for developing comparative data.

4. Arrange the classifications having similar rates of pay into common pay groups for administrative purposes.

5. Develop a pay range plan to accommodate the pay groups developed through the survey and grouping procedure. Use only as many pay grades (ranges) as necessary to display significant differentials in pay between one grouping of jobs having similar rates of pay and another; avoid proliferation. While this is a matter of judgment, arranging the survey data in a scatter diagram format can help determine where significant variations in pay rates occur.

An example of a partial table of pay ranges follows:

Pay Grade	Class Title	Job Titles	Hourly Minimum Rate	Hourly Maximum Rate
1	Food Service Worker	(Pan Washer)		
		(Cook Helper)	$3.25	$3.90
2	Cook	(Pastry Cook)		
		(Salad Cook)		
		(Meat & Vegetable Cook)	3.55	4.25
3	Laborer	(Custodian)		
		(Groundsworker)		
	Clerical Worker	(Clerk Typist)		
		(Clerical Assistant)	3.90	4.70
4	Maintenance Worker	(Equipment Operator)		
		(Building Maintenance Worker)		
	Secretary	(Department Secretary)		
		(Secretary to a Director)	4.30	5.15
5	Crafts Worker	(Carpenter)		
		(Painter)		
		(Electrician)		
		(Plumber)	4.75	5.70

Point Method

This method subdivides each job into several allocation factors, each containing degrees. Each of these degrees has a numerical value (points) assigned to it and the evaluator sums the number of points for each factor to arrive at the value of each job. The difficulty in the point method lies in the identification of factors that are present in all jobs, and in the definition and weighting of the degrees. Allocation factors are not generally weighted equally, as some elements of a job are more important than others. A tenet of wage and salary administration holds that every job can be measured by using four basic allocation factors; skill, effort, responsibility, and working conditions. These four factors, not coincidentally, are reaffirmed in the Equal Pay Act, which requires equal pay for all jobs requiring equal skill, equal effort, and equal responsibility, and are performed under similar working conditions.

Very few point method plans measure jobs by these basic factors alone; rather, each of the four is further expanded into subfactors. Skill, for example, could include education, experience, mental skills, visual skills, and complexity. Effort could be subdivided into mental or physical effort, continuity, and stamina. Responsibility could be subdivided into confidentiality of work, monies handled, and consequences of errors. Working conditions could be broken down into inside or outside assignments, noise levels, travel, and night shifts.

Allocation factors that can be measured are numerous and should be adapted to the needs of each college. One set of factors might be applicable for measuring clerical jobs, another set for food service, custodial, and maintenance work, and another for technical and managerial jobs. The controlling consideration in identifying factors is that *they must be common to the jobs being measured.* If the factors are common, they will no doubt vary in degree. The variance will ultimately reflect the value of each job.

Most clerical jobs can be measured adequately by using the following factors:

1. Job complexity; degree of independent action and the range of difficulty of the tasks to be performed.

2. Personal contacts; responsibility for meeting, dealing with, or influencing other people.

3. Supervision received; degree of control exercised by the immediate supervisor, such as outlining methods to be followed, checking and assigning work, and handling of exceptional cases.

4. Supervision of others; extent and nature of supervisory responsibility.

5. Mental-visual requirements; degree of concentration and coordination of mind and eye, and manual dexterity.

6. Education; minimum required to do the job.

7. Experience; minimum amount, if related experience is required, to perform the job.

8. Effect of errors; their probable effect on the operation of the department or college.

Food service, custodial, and maintenance jobs can be adequately measured by the following factors:

1. Skills required.
2. Education or training required.
3. Experience required.
4. Physical effort required.
5. Responsibility and complexity of the job.

Because the point method permits evaluation of each factor of a job separately, it is generally considered to be more reliable than either the ranking or the classification method. The major disadvantage of the point method is that considerable time and expertise are required to develop a system for using it. Nevertheless, it is the method of job evaluation in widest use today. Small colleges could acquire a point method system from a reliable consultant at relatively low cost, based on the number of employees to be covered.

Following is a step-by-step summary of the point method:

1. Collect information about each job.

2. Identify and define factors that are common to the jobs being measured.

3. Define the factor degrees. This step is based on the premise that jobs vary in the degree to which each factor exists in a job.

4. Determine the relative value of the factors. Only rarely are factors assigned equal weight in determining job values. For example, "entry qualification" will usually be 25% to 35%.

5. Assign point values to the factors and degrees. These are the values that will be used in determining the total point value of the jobs.

6. Rate the jobs.

A brief outline of a point method plan follows:

Factor		Percentage of Total Points
A. Entry Requirements (Education, Training, Experience)		25%
B. Job Content		
Complexity	20%	
Interpersonal Relationships	10%	
Latitude	5%	
Supervision Exercised	10%	
Working Conditions	5%	50%
C. Responsibility and Accountability for Results		25%
		100%

The following table is an example of factor weighting:

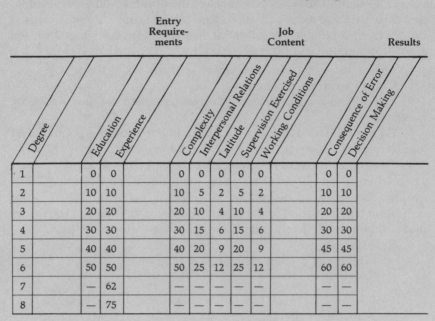

Degree		Entry Requirements			Job Content						Results	
		Education	Experience		Complexity	Interpersonal Relations	Latitude	Supervision Exercised	Working Conditions		Consequence of Error	Decision Making
1		0	0		0	0	0	0	0		0	0
2		10	10		10	5	2	5	2		10	10
3		20	20		20	10	4	10	4		20	20
4		30	30		30	15	6	15	6		30	30
5		40	40		40	20	9	20	9		45	45
6		50	50		50	25	12	25	12		60	60
7		—	62		—	—	—	—	—		—	—
8		—	75		—	—	—	—	—		—	—

Factor Weighting Applied to Jobs*

Factor	Pan Washer	Pastry Cook
Education	0	0
Experience	0	30
Complexity	10	20
Interpersonal Relations	5	5
Latitude	2	4
Supervision Exercised	0	5
Working Conditions	4	4
Consequence of Error	10	30
Decision Making	0	10
Total Points	31	108

Pay Grade I = point range of 0 to 60 points.
Pay Grade II = point range of 61 to 120 points.

In this illustration, the pan washer obviously belongs in the first pay grade, and the pastry cook in Pay Grade II.

*NOTE: This example is for illustrative purposes only. It does not include a definition of degree levels.

Factor Comparison Method

The factor comparison method requires the identification of allocation factors as described under the point method. However, it differs from the point method through the use of bench mark jobs, which are then broken down by factors. Each factor is compared on a job-by-job basis with the bench mark job; that is, the evaluator will evaluate all jobs in terms of one factor, then on the basis of a second factor, and so on until all jobs have been evaluated against all the factors. The points assigned each factor are then summed for each job, thereby determining the relative value of each job.

The factor comparison method has the strong advantage of comparing elements of one job to other jobs to determine relative value. A major disadvantage is the staff expertise and time required to identify bench mark jobs and compensable factors. The factor comparison method ranks second among job evaluation systems used in private industry; however, its use in higher education has been minimal. Although other variations and combinations of job evaluation methods have evolved, each traces its origin essentially to the four traditional plans that are described above.

Market Method

A more recent, nontraditional method of job evaluation is the "market evaluation" method. With the widespread availability of salary survey information, some employers bypass the traditional evaluation approaches and determine their salary schedules from rates paid for comparable work by other employers. The method identifies bench mark jobs for salary comparison purposes; once the salary levels of these jobs are known, others are slotted against them on the basis of difficulty.

The major advantage of this method is that the market is embedded in the program from the outset, thereby reducing variations which sometimes occur when converting the evaluation results to monetary terms. A major disadvantage lies in locating reliable and comparable salary comparison data for bench mark jobs.

Selecting a Job Evaluation Method

When selecting a method of job evaluation, college officers should first consider the availability and expertise of staff to implement and maintain the plan. This directly relates to the complexity of the method selected. For example, the ranking method generally requires limited

time for both implementation and maintenance, but its dubious accept-
ability among employees is a serious drawback.

The classification and point methods usually require greater staff time
for implementation and maintenance than does the ranking method. The
factor comparison method may require still greater staff time and expertise for implementation and maintenance and, consequently, is not recommended for small colleges. It should be emphasized that colleges
should not attempt to install a compensation plan without sufficient staff
expertise or the services of a qualified consultant.

Pay Structure and Pricing

Once the relative difficulty of all jobs has been determined, the next
step is to group similar jobs (those of comparable difficulty or responsibility) into pay grades (wage grades or salary grades). Analysis of the job
evaluation results usually reveals natural clusterings of jobs that are
valuable in deciding the desired number of pay grades; this number
varies among institutions. Colleges should establish only the number of
pay grades necessary to reasonably represent identifiable levels of difficulty. Most small colleges, for example, should limit pay grades for
clerical and secretarial employees to no more than five grades. A college
that permits further proliferation of pay grades will encounter difficulty
in precisely measuring the appropriate grade for a job. As the number of
pay grades increases, the preciseness of assigning comparable jobs to appropriate pay grades decreases.

Rates of pay or salaries should not be allowed to influence the judgment of an evaluator. In most instances when a new salary structure is
installed, the salaries of some employees will not conform to newly established rates or ranges. If the evaluator were to consider the salary of
employees when evaluating the difficulty of a job, he or she could unin-
tentionally determine difficulty based on salaries paid rather than on
duties performed.

Salary Surveys

Jobs generally are priced by using existing wage rates or, more commonly, by the use of wage or salary survey information. The use of salary surveys in setting or adjusting wage rates is recommended because
the surveys reveal rates being paid for key jobs by other employers.
However, if salary surveys are used in setting or adjusting wages and salaries, care must be exercised to determine that survey results actually
cover comparable jobs. For example, one custodian may do nothing but
clean buildings, while another may have watchman duties or mechanical

repair responsibilities. The review of job descriptions rather than job titles helps insure comparability of wage survey information.

A small college may lack the necessary staff to develop and administer its own salary survey, but this does not preclude participation in salary surveys that are conducted by other local employers. In most communities, there are several employers who make regular salary surveys and who would welcome additional employer participation. Telephone companies and other public utilities frequently conduct such surveys. In many communities, the chamber of commerce administers a salary survey and makes the results available to its members. Most salary surveys are conducted in confidence, that is, results are coded so that individual employers are not identified.

Most salary surveys have become comprehensive instruments that solicit data not only on wages and salaries, but also on benefits and personnel practices. This information is indispensible to employers, since it indicates what competitive employers are providing in salaries, benefits, and other practices. (See Exhibit 2D.) The Department of Labor regularly conducts area salary surveys and this information is available to all employers through the local U.S. Employment Service office. The College and University Personnel Association's annual *Administrative Compensation Survey* is recommended as a survey of key exempt jobs. The results of salary surveys should be carefully analyzed and colleges should use this information in making adjustments to their salary ranges. Each college must determine its position in the local labor market.

Wage Rates and Pay Ranges

Rates and ranges represent a conversion of the job evaluation results into monetary terms. Simply stated, the more difficult or complex the job, the higher the wage rate or the pay range. There are clearly advantages and disadvantages to both a single-rate pay plan and a range pay plan. The single-rate pay plan is easier to administer and, in theory, provides "equal pay for equal work." However, it does not provide a means by which employees can be rewarded for performance, length of service, or other considerations. It is viewed by many employees as too structured because it offers no monetary incentive for doing a better job.

Pay range programs afford the employees monetary growth and rewards based on performance, length of service, etc. If performance is incorporated as a factor for determining pay increases, it requires structure and consistent administration. Performance increases are subjective considerations and may be viewed negatively by employees if they are not allocated in a consistent manner.

Pay ranges are usually constructed to include a minimum and a maximum salary. The width of the pay range—the spread between the minimum and the maximum—varies by two primary factors: types of jobs and number of pay grades or levels. In unskilled and semi-skilled jobs, this variation usually runs from 15% to 25%. In skilled jobs the ranges vary 20% to 30% and in administrative work, from 30% to 50%. These are general guidelines, however, and actual ranges could vary even further.

Ranges are usually constructed to incorporate an "overlapping feature," that is, the *maximum* of range one is more than the *minimum* of range two, and so on. This overlapping feature is used to reward longevity and to minimize the pressure for reclassification of a job to the next higher range solely because the employee's salary has reached the maximum of the range. Most colleges adjust their pay ranges annually, generally maintaining the same range width, which necessitates alteration in both minimum and maximum of the range.

Scatter Diagram

The scatter diagram or scattergram is a graphic tool used in wage and salary administration to plot pay ranges. It is constructed by designing a simple graph with horizontal and vertical planes. Pay rates are located on the vertical axis and points or pay grades on the horizontal axis. Actual rates of pay and points or pay grades are then plotted on the chart at the appropriate location. After all jobs have been plotted, a trend line is drawn through the graph and it is analyzed to construct range widths.

"Red Circle" Rates

When a new pay plan is installed, existing pay rates, as noted earlier, will not always conform to the new ranges; some will fall below the minimum and some will exceed the maximum. These are referred to as "red circle" rates. Rates that fall below the range are usually adjusted upward to at least the minimum of the new range either immediately on its implementation or over a short subsequent period. Pay that exceeds the maximum of the range may be handled in several ways: (1) the employee's current salary may be frozen until the maximum of the range catches up with that salary; (2) the employee's salary may be permitted to remain at the same dollar or percentage differential beyond the range maximum for the duration of the employment relationship, so long as the employee remains in the same job or pay grade level. The latter method or some variation of it is preferred, because it has less monetary impact on affected employees.

High Entry Salary Maximums

In recent years, some employers have utilized a "high entry salary maximum" concept to protect incumbent employees from new employees entering the pay range at rates in excess of incumbents. If, for example, a salary range has a spread of 40%, that is, the maximum is 40% greater than the minimum, new employees would be limited to a starting salary not greater than an amount 10% into the range. This 10% rate represents the "high entry salary maximum" for new employees. The concept affords an employer the necessary flexibility to hire new employees at a rate beyond the minimum, based on their education and experience; yet, it has the advantage of limiting the new rate. This factor has become an important influence on employee morale because incumbent employees may resent new employees being hired at pay rates equal to or in excess of their own.

Automatic and Merit Progression

Once pay ranges have been established, employers usually determine progression through the ranges by two methods, automatic or longevity progression and merit progression. The automatic progression provides salary increases at specified intervals, for example, on an anniversary date, based solely on length of service. The merit progression provides salary increases based on proficiency or quality of performance; the increases serve as an incentive and reward for meritorious performance.

Several variations of these features evolved in the 1960s and 1970s, the most popular of which combines the two by providing automatic progression to the midpoint of the range and merit progression from the midpoint to the maximum.

Step Rates and Open Range

The step rate, sometimes called "lock-step," has been used for a number of years. Steps become the vehicle for granting increases within a range. To use this approach, intervals are strategically selected within the range and salary increases are granted in specified amounts equal to the steps. For example, if a range is from $3.15 to $3.75 per hour, step increases could be established at $3.30, $3.45, $3.60, and $3.75. The number and size of steps will vary with the width of the range. Ranges usually contain no fewer than three and not more than seven steps. The step concept is equally adaptable for automatic, merit, or combination progression plans. (Performance appraisal plans, which are prerequisites for merit progression plans, are described in Chapter 4.)

The open range approach, as the name implies, permits progression through the range without regard to the specific salary increment that characterizes step plans. When a merit progression concept is used in an open range, supervisors are generally accorded flexibility when allocating salary increases based on performance. Merit increases, for example, could vary from 4% to 8% with the open range approach, whereas the step approach would require increases to conform to designated steps. Some employers have introduced flexibility into their step plans by allowing for double-step increases for outstanding performance. The open-range approach appears to be more suitable for small colleges because of its flexibility during periods of high inflation and scarce resources.

Across-the-Board Adjustment

Many compensation plans in higher education incorporate some form of across-the-board adjustment. Usually, salary increases are given to all employees at the beginning of the fiscal year. These increases may be based on a fixed percentage for all employees or the percentage may vary by major employee group. The across-the-board adjustment is generally designed to be a partial replacement for lost purchasing power and has frequently been used as a substitute for cost-of-living increases which are common in industry.

The cost-of-living concept relates salary increases to upward adjustments in the Consumer Price Index. Very few colleges use cost-of-living plans because of their enormous cost. Most institutions offer annual salary increases, which are a partial offset to the increased cost of living.

Minimum Wage

The recent increases in the federal minimum wage have been costly for many institutions of higher education. In addition to the direct dollar cost of compliance, the law has affected the rate-range wage structure of many colleges. Wage adjustments for employees whose rates are below the prescribed minimum may compact the wage rates for employees whose rates are above the minimum. Ideally, a wage adjustment should be given to employees whose rates are above the minimum, similar to that for employees whose rates are below, but such adjustments would probably strain an institution's resources. However, if no adjustment is made, workforce morale may deteriorate, particularly in light of the prevailing pattern of making sizable adjustments to the minimum wage on an annual basis.

If an institution does not have sufficient resources to adjust all rates and ranges, there is a modified approach that can be applied on a short-term basis. The rates at or just above the minimum wage require the most careful attention. Employees receiving these rates generally measure them against the minimum wage. By adjusting these rates on a sliding scale, that is, by applying a smaller increase to those farthest away from the minimum wage, the impact is reduced. This approach also provides employees a psychological benefit because it demonstrates the institution's concern for their pay rates. The additional expenditure of dollars to implement this approach can produce valuable results in stabilized morale and decreased employee turnover.

Salary Increases for Promotions

Criteria in pay plans that cover salary increases must be developed with great care. Above all, salary increase policies for promotions must be equitable. If employees view such increases as inequitable because new employees performing the same job receive higher salaries, they will become frustrated. Although amounts vary from pay plan to pay plan and even within pay plans based on ranges and steps, increases for promotions should be at least 5%. Increases that fall below 5% generally do not provide a sufficient reward for the assumption of additional responsibilities and may cause morale problems.

Communicating Compensation Policy and Procedures

A college should take great pains to communicate compensation policy and procedures to its employees, including supervisors. A well-intentioned and equitable compensation plan can be judged inequitable and fail to win acceptance if its concepts and principles are misunderstood by employees. Employee suspicion of a compensation plan can be eliminated by sharing it openly. Plans, policies, and procedures can be distributed to employees through a separate booklet or through inclusion in a personnel policy and procedures manual or handbook. Such a publication need not be lengthy; the essential information can be sufficiently described in ten to twenty pages.

Compensation Plan; Maintenance and Control

Once a compensation plan has been installed, it must be maintained. Failure to do this produces many of the problems that are characteristic of an informal, paternalistic pay plan.

Position descriptions should be reviewed on a regular basis to insure that compensation is commensurate with the duties and responsibilities involved. In a small college, where personnel staffing is insufficient to permit regular reviews of jobs by a job analyst, all position descriptions should be submitted to the compensation administrator for review once a year. Each department can be instructed in writing to update the job descriptions of employees and to submit them to the personnel or business office within one month. The updated job descriptions should then be reviewed and analyzed to determine whether or not the job is properly classified. (See Exhibit 2E.)

New positions must be integrated into the compensation plan. Frequently, supervisors lack the necessary information to write a detailed position description for a new job, which makes it difficult to determine the appropriate classification of the job. Such information may be obtained through the use of a new position description questionnaire. (See Exhibit 2F.)

Adjustment of the pay structure is a necessary maintenance task, which in colleges is usually annual, coinciding with the fiscal year. The salary survey process described earlier in this chapter is the primary toc' available for evaluaton of external, or competitive, pay rates. A rev' of employees' salaries by classification or pay grade may provide va. able insight into internal pay inequities that should be corrected. Exit interviews (discussed in Chapter 1) may also reveal pay problems. The money available, of course, ultimately becomes the primary constraint for adjusting the pay structure. However, failure to use other tools suggested here may mean that problems or potential problems will go undiscovered or unresolved.

Pay rates are directly affected, both internally and externally, by the supply and demand aspects of the labor markets. Unfortunately, these aspects are not distributed equally among all jobs. Salary surveys, turnover analyses, exit interviews, and review of employees' salaries within ranges will assist colleges in identifying labor market fluctuations and in making pay structure adjustments.

The information in this chapter is a summary of the wage and salary options available to college administrators. Implementation of a formalized compensation plan should be undertaken only after careful study under the guidance of a knowledgeable wage and salary practitioner or of a consultant.

Exhibit 2A₁

Job Analysis Questionnaire

INSTRUCTIONS: The purpose of this questionnaire is to gather information to be used in determining a specific title and pay range for the position. Please relate the information you give to the position itself—not to the individual who is currently holding the position. Someone thoroughly familiar with the position should complete this form. If this is a request only to add or delete a clerical skill (typing or shorthand), it is not necessary to complete this form—a memo to Personnel Services signed by the department head will suffice. This information may be supplemented by personal interviews and observation. Please call Personnel Services if you have questions.

PLEASE TYPE CHECK ONE (✔)	☐ Request for reclassification (This form should be completed by the incumbent and approved by the budget unit head.)	Date:
	☐ Request for a new position (To be completed by budget unit head or supervisor)	Date:

Incumbent's Name	Current Position Title	Position Number
Department	Account Number	Telephone

A. JOB FUNCTION STATEMENT (Brief summary of overall responsibility.)

[add lines as necessary]

B. SIMPLE ORGANIZATIONAL CHART (Illustrating Supervision Given/Received)

[add space as necessary]

C. SUPERVISION GIVEN/RECEIVED (Explain reporting relationships illustrated above)

[add lines as necessary]

D. JOB DESCRIPTION— (Provide a detailed listing of duties performed on the job and specific percentages of time, avoiding general statements such as "typing," "filing," "keeping records," etc. Action verbs such as "coordinates," "prepares," and "directs" should be explained.)

% OF TIME	REGULARLY PERFORMED DUTIES
	[add lines as necessary]

D. JOB DESCRIPTION— CONTINUED—(List irregularly performed duties. These duties should be performed on occasion rather than monthly, weekly, or daily and may not be directly related to the regular duties.)

% OF TIME	OCCASIONAL OR IRREGULAR DUTIES
	[add lines as necessary]

E. OBJECTIVE OF REVIEW(To be completed by supervisor. Explain need for new position, reorganization, additions, deletions or changes to job.)

[add lines as necessary]

	Date Position Last Reviewed

F. MINIMUM QUALIFICATIONS (To be completed by supervisor.)

Education:

Experience:

Skills:

Others:

Signature of Department Head		Signature of Person Preparing Description	
PERSONNEL OFFICE USE ONLY	Recommended Classification	Analyst	Date
	Classification	Approved	Date

Exhibit 2A$_2$

Job Analysis Classification Questionnaire
PERSONNEL SERVICES

(Please print or type)

☐ REQUEST FOR CLASSIFICATION OF NEW POSITION. *(Entire form to be prepared by Supervisor or Department Head and approved by Dean or Director.)*

☐ REQUEST FOR RECLASSIFICATION. *(Page 1, 2, and 3 to be filled out by employee and page 4 by Supervisor or Department Head with approval of Dean or Director.*

1. LAST NAME–FIRST NAME–MIDDLE NAME		
2. PRESENT JOB TITLE	DEPARTMENT	
3. LOCATION *(Building)*	ROOM NO.	TELEPHONE
4. SUPERVISOR'S NAME	TITLE	

5. HOURS OF WORK FROM TO	REGULAR WORK DAYS	SATURDAY AND SUNDAY HOURS	TOTAL HOURS PER WEEK
6. HOW LONG HAVE YOUR DUTIES AND RESPONSIBILITIES BEEN SUBSTANTIALLY AS SHOWN BELOW?		7. IN YOUR OPINION, WHAT SHOULD BE YOUR JOB TITLE?	

8. Using your own words, describe IN DETAIL the work you do. Use additional sheets if necessary. Under the column "% OF TIME," estimate approximately the time you devote to duties listed. Use great care to give a clear and complete statement.

% OF TIME	DESCRIPTION OF DUTIES
	A. REGULAR DUTIES *(Duties performed daily or almost daily, such as typing letters, taking dictation, instructing other employees, planning menus, stocking shelves, etc.)*
	B. PERIODIC DUTIES *(Duties performed at recurring fixed intervals, such as preparation of annual budgets, checking inventory, designing forms, etc.)*

% OF TIME	DESCRIPTION OF DUTIES
	C. OCCASIONAL OR IRREGULAR DUTIES: *(Duties of a nonrecurring nature, such as designing forms, assisting at special events, shoveling snow, etc.)*

9. LIST MACHINES YOU USE IN YOUR WORK *(such as typewriter, calculator, milling machine, etc.)*

10. ARE YOU RESPONSIBLE FOR CASH, EXPENSIVE EQUIPMENT, OR SUPPLIES?
☐ Yes *(Explain)* ☐ No

11. DO YOU ASSEMBLE INFORMATION AND PREPARE REPORTS AND SUMMARIES THEREFROM?
☐ Yes *(Explain)* ☐ No

12. INDICATE HOW MUCH PHYSICAL STRENGTH AND STAMINA YOUR JOB REQUIRES AND WHAT AS-PECTS OF YOUR JOB REQUIRE THEM. ARE THERE ANY PERIODS OF RUSH LOAD?

13. STATE THE TYPE, EXTENT, FREQUENCY OF CONTACT YOU HAVE WITH, OR OF ASSISTANCE YOU REN-DER TO, THE FOLLOWING:
A. Other Departments.

B. Students.

C. Academic Staff.

D. Public.

14.　　A. DO YOU SUPERVISE OTHER EMPLOYEES?
☐ Yes *(List number of people that you supervise by NAME and TITLE.)* ☐ No

B. INDICATE THE TYPE OF SUPERVISION GIVEN TO OTHERS. *(For example, complete overall supervision, Including hiring; salary recommendations; assign work; give instructions for handling assigned work; verify or check work performed.)*

_____

_____

_____

C. WHAT PERCENTAGE OF TIME DO YOU SPEND IN PLANNING OR DIRECTING THE WORK OF OTHERS?

_____

_____

15. A. FROM WHOM DO YOU RECEIVE INSTRUCTIONS OR WORK ASSIGNMENTS?

  B. HOW FREQUENTLY DO YOU RECEIVE INSTRUCTIONS OR WORK ASSIGNMENTS?

_____

_____

  C. IN WHAT FORM DO YOU RECEIVE INSTRUCTIONS OR WORK ASSIGNMENTS? *(Oral instructions, penciled layout, rough draft, blueprints, etc.)*

_____

16. HOW IS YOUR WORK CHECKED OR REVIEWED? *(For example, all work is checked, spot-checked, or reviewed for overall results.)*

_____

_____

17. WHAT KIND OF DECISIONS DO YOU MAKE WITHOUT REFERRING TO HIGHER AUTHORITY?

_____

18. ARE YOU RESPONSIBLE FOR ORIGINATING OR ADOPTING POLICIES, PROCEDURES, PLANS, AND PROGRAMS?
 ☐ Yes *(Explain)* ☐ No

_____

_____

19. DOES YOUR JOB INVOLVE EMERGENCY OR ON-CALL SERVICE?
 ☐ Yes   ☐ No *If answer is "yes," explain whether:* ☐ Regular ☐ Occasional ☐ Seasonal
 Describe and estimate amount involved.

_____

20. WHAT DO YOU CONSIDER THE MOST DIFFICULT OR DEMANDING PART OF YOUR JOB?

_____

_____

21. GIVE A BRIEF SUMMARY OF YOUR POSITION.

_____

_____

DATE	SIGNATURE

STATEMENT OF IMMEDIATE SUPERVISOR

22. PLEASE COMMENT ON EMPLOYEE'S STATEMENT, INDICATE ANY MODIFICATIONS, ADDITIONS OR DIFFERENCE IN EMPHASIS.

23. WHAT DO YOU CONSIDER THE MOST IMPORTANT DUTIES AND RESPONSIBILITIES OF THIS POSITION?

24. HOW ARE INSTRUCTIONS ISSUED FOR THIS POSITION? INDICATE IN WHAT FORM, IN WHAT DETAIL, HOW FREQUENTLY.

25. WHAT SUPERVISION AND ATTENTION IS GIVEN THE EMPLOYEE IN THIS POSITION?

26. ASSUMING A NEW EMPLOYEE POSSESSES BASIC QUALIFICATIONS FOR THE POSITION, INDICATE HOW LONG A BREAK-IN PERIOD WOULD BE REQUIRED.

| DATE | SIGNATURE |
| | TITLE |

STATEMENT OF DEPARTMENT HEAD

27. Indicate the qualifications which you think should be required in filling a FUTURE vacancy in this position. Keep the position itself in mind, rather than the qualifications of the individual who now occupies it.

	MINIMUM QUALIFICATIONS	ADDITIONAL DESIRABLE QUALIFICATIONS
Education, General		
Education, Special or Professional		
Experience, Length in Years and Kind		
Licenses, Certificates, or Registrations		
Special Knowledge, Abilities and Skills		

28. GENERAL COMMENTS *(Use additional sheets, if necessary.)*

29. WHAT TITLE DO YOU FEEL IS MOST APPROPRIATE FOR THE ABOVE DESCRIBED POSITION?

| DATE | SIGNATURE |
| | TITLE |

DEAN OR ADMINISTRATIVE OFFICER

30. GENERAL COMMENTS *(Use additional sheets, if necessary.)*

| DATE | SIGNATURE |
| | TITLE |

(Please return completed questionnaire to the Campus Personnel Office)

Exhibit 2B₁

Position Description
Academic Buildings

Job Title: JANITORIAL WORKER

The following description includes the most significant duties performed but does not exclude other occasional work assignments that are not mentioned. Work is performed under general supervision.

1. Collect trash from all offices, classrooms, and lavatories, and remove trash from building.
2. Clean all offices.
   Empty wastebaskets and empty and damp-wipe ash trays. Dust all furniture and horizontal surfaces: desks, tables, chairs, sofas, ledges, files, bookcases, cabinets, hat and coat racks, window sills, baseboards, radiator covers, telephones, fire extinguishers, etc. Clean glass doors and drinking fountains. Wipe up spillage on furniture and floors. Dust-mop floors and vacuum entire carpets. Spot-clean furniture, walls, and doors.
3. Clean all Classrooms and Laboratories.
   Empty wastebaskets and empty and damp-wipe ash trays. Clean chalkboards and chalk rails. Dust tables, chairs, desks, sills, ledges, radiator covers, etc. Clean glass doors and drinking fountains. Wipe up spillage on furniture and floors. Dust-mop entire floor. Damp-mop as needed. Spot-clean furniture and walls. Straighten chairs.
4. Clean all Washrooms.
   Sweep or police floor if litter is present. Damp-dust and spot-clean all ledges, walls, doors, sills, radiator covers, dispensers, stalls, cabinets, pipes, etc. Clean mirrors. Clean and disinfect all surfaces—tops, sides, and underneath—of washbasins, commodes, urinals, and all attached hardware and fixtures, and dry chrome hardware to prevent water spotting. On inside of commodes and urinals, use acid bowl-cleaner at least once weekly to prevent buildup of mineral deposits. Check and fill dispensers. Damp-mop floor.
5. Dust and damp-mop all halls and stairways.
6. Frequently use 12-inch, 15-inch, 17-inch, and 19-inch floor machine for corridor buffing, floor reconditioning, and floor finish stripping.
7. Wash windows (inside and out), using 4-foot to 6-foot ladder.
8. Frequently replace light bulbs from 4-foot to 6-foot ladder.
9. Perform other duties similar to or related to the type described above.

Position Description

Job Title: GROUNDSKEEPER

The following description covers the most significant duties performed but does not exclude other occasional work assignments not mentioned.

1. Daily policing of campus areas (first thing each morning).
2. Grass cutting and trimming (power mowers and hand tools).
3. Weeding (flower beds, around shrubs, and any other areas where weeding is required).
4. Removal of leaves (by rake or power equipment).
5. Trimming and shaping of trees and shrubs.
6. Removal of branches, wood, and tree stumps from campus areas when necessary.
7. Snow and ice removal (hand tools, power equipment, and chemicals). This may require working overtime, nights, early morning, weekends, or holidays.
8. Because of inclement weather, may be required to do other work not pertaining to grounds, such as help in maintenance work, hauling, moving and storing of furniture, equipment, and supplies. Cleaning of storage areas, etc., included.
9. Keep a groundswork log showing work area, date, time started, time completed, and a description of the job.
10. Perform other duties similar or related to the type described above.

Classification Specification

Title: SECRETARY I   *Grade:*   3

Position Summary.   Under close supervision, performs general, routine, and elementary secretarial duties.

Supervision and Direction Received.   Receives specific directions from, and work is closely reviewed by, a higher-level secretary or an office or department manager.

Supervision and Direction Exercised.   None.

Machines and Equipment Used.   Typewriter, voice recording equipment, adding machine, calculating machine, office copiers.

Typical Duties.

1. Receives mail, makes general sort, and distributes by department office or areas.

2. Types routine correspondence and reports from recorded dictation, rough-typed draft, or manuscript. Types entries on departmental forms and the like.
3. Sorts and files correspondence, reports, and the like.
4. May accumulate and record repetitive information and statistics.
5. As an occasional or regular added duty, may serve as receptionist: receiving, announcing, and routing visitors and telephone calls; providing limited information, and the like.
6. Assists in other general and limited office duties.

Qualifications.
Education: Completion of high school with some instruction in business subjects.
Experience: None.
Technical: The ability to type accurately at 35 to 40 words per minute from recorded dictation or handwritten copy.
OR—a combination of formal training and experience equivalent to the above.

Exhibit 2C₂   **Classification Specification**

Title: SECRETARY II   *Grade:*   5

Position Summary.   With specific direction and supervision, performs routine and nonroutine office duties requiring general secretarial skills and proficiency. May concentrate on secretarial duties in a particular discipline involving specialized and complicated terminology, vocabulary, and abbreviations.

Supervision and Direction Received.   Receives specific direction from office supervisor, department head, or higher level secretaries.

Supervision and Direction Exercised.   May be responsible for the assignment of routine work to, and review of completed work of, other clerical assistants in the office, such as file clerks, beginning record clerks, and typists.

Machines and Equipment Used.   Typewriter, voice recording equipment, adding machine, calculating machine, office copiers.

Typical Duties.
1. Receives, opens, scans, sorts, and routes incoming mail for information or response.

2. Types and transcribes dictation (oral or recorded). Types from rough, longhand drafts.
3. Occasionally composes and types nonroutine correspondence for approval and signature.
4. Accumulates records and types standardized reports and forms. May set up and type special department reports and forms.
5. May perform department receptionist duties in addition to secretarial duties.
6. As a specialized secretary, types from voice recorders and handwritten notes a considerable volume of reports, histories, summaries, and records involving specialized and complicated terminology, vocabulary, and abbreviations.
7. Maintains general office filing systems and may set up and maintain special files.
8. Orders and controls office supplies and materials.
9. Performs other related general secretarial duties.

Qualifications.

Education: Completion of high school, plus two years of postsecondary education—preferably in secretarial studies, or equivalent work experience (see below).

Experience: None, with required education background (see above), *or* two years of practical secretarial or office experience after completion of high school.

Technical: The ability to type from draft or recorded dictation accurately at 55 words per minute. The ability to operate commonly used office machines, such as voice recording equipment, adding machine, office copiers, etc. The ability to take dictation is desirable but not required.
OR—a combination of formal training and experience equivalent to the above.

Exhibit 2D

How To Conduct a Salary Survey

The following article was prepared by James M. Wagner, of the Pennsylvania State University, for the "How-to" series published by the College and University Personnel Association.

A salary survey enables an institution to compare its rates of pay for similar work with other organizations in the area. The survey data can be of assistance in determining required amounts for general salary increases and how much the institution must offer to be competitive for particular skills.

The first step is to determine the institutional salary policy. That is, will the institution pay average, above average, or below average rates in its recruiting area?

Which Geographical Areas Should Be Surveyed?

The salary survey should encompass the labor market in which the college recruits. This varies by type of job. A good way to determine the general reach of the labor market is to screen institutional hiring records for the last year to find where the bulk of new employees are coming from by type of job. For example, if recruiting janitorial workers, the labor market would be in the immediate area. On the other hand, if recruiting a director of purchasing, the market area might well be the entire United States.

Which Organizations Should Be Surveyed?

Identify the organizations with which the college or university competes in recruiting employees. These organizations must have jobs that are similar to those in the institution in order to make valid comparisons. The number of organizations surveyed largely depends on time and resources available. However, ten to fifteen well-selected companies will provide valid statistical data on which to base recommendations.

Selection of "Bench Mark" Jobs

It is not feasible to survey every job title in an organization. Therefore, it is necessary to select "bench mark" jobs. A bench mark job is one that will provide a representative sampling of a group of jobs. For example, from an entire personnel department, four jobs might be selected—a personnel supervisor, a job analyst, a senior health insurance clerk, and a clerk-typist. These four jobs provide a representative sample. Be careful that jobs picked are common to most organizations being surveyed and that they provide a good cross section of all types of jobs. A perfect match is not always possible, but the jobs to be compared should be similar in most respects. The importance of the selection of bench mark jobs cannot be overemphasized, as it has a definite bearing on the success of the survey.

Too many job samples will be a burden to those participating because of the time and effort required to assemble the necessary information. It may cause them to become careless and to provide incorrect salary data. Project yourself to the other side of the survey and consider whether *you* would (1) provide the requested information; (2) reply kindly, but negatively; or (3) throw the request in the wastepaper basket. Many people make a salary survey so detailed and complex that most organizations do not have the requested information readily available and therefore do not participate.

Preparation of Descriptions

Job titles can be misleading; matching them should never be considered as a method of conducting a salary survey. In order to compare apples with apples and oranges with oranges, a brief, concise description of the duties and responsibilities for each bench mark job selected must be prepared. These descriptions should be provided to each organization surveyed in order to insure comparability. They should include those elements needed to make such comparisons. For example, education and experience requirements are essential in making accurate comparisons.

What Rates Should Be Requested?

Be careful that the rates requested are rates commonly used. Service and trades-related jobs are normally paid on an hourly basis, clerical jobs may be weekly, and staff employees may be compensated on a monthly basis. Allow participating organizations to choose the form of salary information they will supply. This may require a simple mathematical conversion on your part, but will lessen the burden of preparation for the participating party. Such conversions should be based on hours worked per week. Generally, the "hiring" and "going" rate are sufficient for service and trades-related jobs, and a minimum, midpoint, and maximum are usually available for clerical and staff employees. You may wish to request the average rate paid most employees on a particular job.

What Kinds of Contacts Should Be Made?

To be most effective, the survey should be handled on a person-to-person basis. Telephone is next best. Surveys conducted solely by mail frequently produce poor results. The survey should be mailed in advance and preparation for your visit or call should include a list of questions reduced to writing, such as:

1. How many employees are in the various classifications being surveyed?
2. What are the effective dates of the salary information provided?
3. Do you have union affiliations? If so, have you negotiated future rates? What are they?
4. What is your forecast of scheduled wage and salary increases?
5. How many hours of work per week are required?
6. How many paid holidays are provided?
7. What health and life insurance benefits are provided?
8. What paid vacation and sick leave benefits are provided?
9. What type of longevity increments do you provide?

Keep constantly in mind the person who must gather the information. Don't ask for information unless it is absolutely necessary. Keep it simple! The person making the contact should have sufficient organizational stature to have access to confidential salaries in the organization, thus insuring comparison and transfer of reliable data. A personal visit can insure confidentiality.

Tabulation of Results

After the results of the survey have been tabulated and summarized, the information presented by each participant should be coded and distributed to the participants, giving them only the code letters assigned to their organization. Normally, it is permissible to disclose to cooperating organizations the names of those participating in the survey, but not their code numbers without specific written permission.

The salary survey summary should be shared with participants as promptly after completion as possible. The summary should include:

1. A coded list of all bench mark jobs surveyed in each organization, with the applicable rates.
2. Explanation of the nature of the salary information presented.
3. Interpretation of the results.
4. Note of appreciation for assistance given.

Exhibit 2E

How To Keep Classifications Current Through Regular Review

The following article was prepared by Kenneth D. Oswald, of the University of Utah, for the "How-to" series published by the College and University Personnel Association.

The many benefits of a good job classification system are easily eroded unless the system embodies periodic review of the classifications of individual positions. Positions often change. A new employee may make the position something it previously was not. A new supervisor may realign work assignments so that the class to which a position was originally assigned is incorrect at a later date. A regular review of staff positions helps locate these situations and provides an opportunity to keep job descriptions and job understanding up-to-date.

The Job Analyst

The individual responsible for a classification review program is determined by size of the organization, the extent to which a classification system has been implemented, and various other factors, including budget limitations. A large university, with a partially established classification system, may employ job analysts, who review previously classified jobs and also expand the classification system. A smaller college may wish to assign classification review to a current staff member. The job analyst position can be an entry-level position for a recent graduate, if ongoing training is available. However, more sophisticated personnel organizations may seek analysts with previous experience or specialized training.

The Use of Questionnaires

A classification review program works most effectively if the employees whose positions are to be reviewed first complete a carefully designed questionnaire. The analyst can better compare positions and cover more ground in less time if questionnaires are used. These can be useful for the personnel department when seeking replacements for appropriate jobs, and to a supervisor when training a replacement.

It is often desirable to have different questionnaires for different job families. The questionnaires for jobs of an office nature should emphasize such items as level of contact, decision-making requirements, and accountability. Nonoffice-job questionnaires should ask questions that relate to such areas as working conditions, supervisory responsibilities, and equipment use and care. The last page of a questionnaire should be reserved for the supervisor's comments. Questions may include those relating to the supervisor's assessment of an employee's statements on the preceding pages, to the recommendations of qualifications for the position, and to the way this position is ranked in relation to others that are supervised.

A cover letter can be attached to each questionnaire. This letter should explain the purpose of the questionnaire, give suggestions about its completion, and indicate deadlines for submitting the completed questionnaire to the supervisor and for returning it to the personnel department. It also may be emphasized in the cover letter that the results of the project will in no way jeopardize the employee's current salary (assuming this is organization policy).

Approach to Classification Review

Planning is an essential part of classification review. It must first be determined whether the approach should be by department or by function (all jobs having closely related functions, such as an accounting clerk series, reviewed regardless of their location within the organization).

The departmental approach, in which all of the positions within a particular unit are reviewed at the same time, normally permits a better understanding of the interrelationships of the various jobs in the unit and may require fewer on-the-job conferences with the supervisor. The functional approach allows the analyst to compare all jobs of closely related classes at the same time, but may require several visits to the same area as the different campuswide classes are reviewed.

In either approach, the development and use of organization charts will provide visual understanding of department structure and assist in establishing relationships. Once the approach has been determined, specific goals and objectives should be established. A calendar showing the dates by which the various department or position classifications will be reviewed is helpful.

Process of the Review

Following the planning and organization phase, the step-by-step process for classification review should include:

1. Personal visits with unit supervisors to solicit their cooperation and to leave the questionnaires for distribution among their employees. These visits can also be used for discussions on job classification principles. The discussions should stress how the system helps insure internal equity and external competitiveness in pay for employees.

2. A specific date for obtaining the complete questionnaires from the supervisors.

3. A review of the completed questionnaires, preparation of job descriptions, and evaluation of the positions using the existing job evaluation method.

4. An audit of the information contained on the questionnaire with the appropriate employee, if there is some question regarding the information provided on the questionnaire.

5. A summary of the results of the review with the supervisor. This may be done through correspondence, but another visit is suggested if extensive changes in classification are made.

6. Updating the personnel records, where changes in the job description or position classification have been made.

Once all positions encompassed by the classification system have been reviewed, it will probably be time to start over again! This time it may be sufficient to request each supervisor to review the complete job descriptions which are only a year or two old and make any necessary changes. The analyst can then review the changes and make any necessary classification adjustments. In order for the review to be effective, changes that develop should be implemented in accordance with good personnel practices and within budgetary limitations.

Exhibit 2F

	DO NOT WRITE IN THIS SPACE
	Job Title:
New Position Description QUESTIONNAIRE	Classification:
	Salary Grade:
	Salary Range:
Prepare a separate description for each new position requested. Forward original copy only to this department.	Recommended By:

1. Suggested Job Title	2. Department	3. Date of Request

4. Who will be the immediate superior for this position?
Name: Title:

5. SUPERVISION GIVEN TO OTHERS. Give the following information about other positions the incumbent would exercise supervision over.
Attach an additional sheet if more space is needed.

Title	Name	Nature of Supervision

6. DESCRIPTION OF DUTIES. Describe the work in sufficient detail to give a clear word picture of the job.

Percent of Total Time	Describe the more important or time-consuming duties first. Use separate paragraphs for each kind of work. In the left column, estimate how total working time is divided.
	[add space as necessary]

7. What qualifications should be required for this position?

    A. Minimum Educational Requirements:

        Grammar school_____years

        High school_____years, majoring in _____

        Vocational school, with training in field of_____

        Business college or partial college (1-2 years) specializing in_____

        College (graduate), majoring in_____

        University, graduate study for_____years, majoring in_____

B. Minimum Experience: (List amounts and type)

C. Essential knowledge, skills, and abilities:

D. Licenses:

8. Remarks: Submit any other information not covered above. Attach additional sheet if needed.

9. Supervisor: I certify that the answers to the foregoing questions are correct to the best of my knowledge.

Date: Title: Signature:

10. Dean, Director, or his representative: The above statements are accurate and complete. I am satisfied to have this position classified on the basis of the information given.

Date: Title: Signature:

NOTE: *As an alternative, a job analysis or description form, filled out by a supervisor, could be used instead of the "New Position Description" questionnaire to fill the requirements illustrated in this exhibit.*

3. benefits

Employers have traditionally referred to nonwage compensation items as "fringe benefits." A trend has developed, however, to omit the term "fringe" and to refer to such compensation as "benefits programs"; this is a result of the growing awareness of employers that benefits are an integral part of their overall compensation program. Employers must provide benefits that are comprehensive, as well as competitive, in order to attract and retain competent employees.

The employer's cost of offering an essential benefits program has increased significantly during the 1970s and will probably continue to rise in the years ahead. The out-of-pocket cost for benefit programs, that is, for all insurance, retirement contributions, and paid time for not working, (vacations, holidays, etc,) usually ranges upward from 20% of the salary budget for colleges, depending on the types of programs and the nature of coverage.

Benefits are usually presented in formal policy statements concerning vacation and other types of leave; insurance coverages, such as hospital-medical-surgical and life; and retirement programs. Institutions often find it necessary to expand or otherwise modify their benefits programs to remain competitive. Such a program requires continual, systematic review of complex information, reports, and trends, in order to insure that it is cost-effective and competitive. Many colleges retain consultants to assist in benefits planning and programming in order to make the best choices among the various options and coverages available.

Communication of Benefits

A comprehensive benefits package includes many detailed facts, on items such as coverages, exclusions, and regulations, which frequently are not understood by employees. Effective communication of benefits is therefore necessary. It is important that employees know the intricacies of the various benefits plans and their costs. Frequently, colleges communicate the former, but neglect the latter.

Information concerning a benefits program should be disseminated through employee handbooks, bulletins or letters, and the legal plan documents that describe essential details. Employees generally fail to concern themselves with such details until a need arises, but this does not indicate that benefits should be communicated only on a need-to-know basis.

An excellent means of reinforcing the benefits-communication process is to cover different elements of the program in brief articles in the college house organ. If there is none, an attachment to a regularly published calendar of institutional events is a good alternative. Such communications are generally well read by faculty and staff, and information on the benefits and on their cost to the college can be effectively delivered at the same time. Information on benefits should be presented periodically to faculty and staff through written communications, workshops, meetings, or preferably a combination of these.

Individual Benefits Statements

The "individual benefits statement," or "personal annual report" is a useful tool in communicating basic benefits and related costs. Such statements have grown in popularity primarily because of the Employee Retirement Income and Security Act of 1974 (ERISA), and because computer and word processing services have made their production more efficient and reasonable. Some institutions use a computerized benefits statement for each faculty and staff member and mail these annually to their homes. Software packages for payroll and personnel are available from various vendors, or statements can be designed by the personnel or benefits department "in house" with the cooperation of the college computer center.

An individual benefits statement generally includes salary information, brief explanations of insurance coverage and amounts, pension and annuity data, and vacation and sick leave balances. The employer's cost is also indicated, as a percentage of salary, which demonstrates to employees that benefits equal a certain percentage of salary. It is recommended that information of this type be sent to the employee's home so that it can be read by the employee's spouse, to reinforce communication. Abbreviated benefits statements can be produced manually on an annual basis at minimal cost to the institution. (See Exhibits $3A_1$ and $3A_2$.)

This chapter describes a typical college benefits program under three sections: noninsured benefits, insured benefits, and statutory programs.

Noninsured Benefits

The typical benefits accorded college employees are generally allocated in an institution's "personal services" budget, since these benefits relate to compensation and have recurring application. Institutional policy statements that formulate such programs usually incorporate "eligibility criteria" and occasionally restrictions or conditions on the use of benefits.

Holidays

Paid holidays traditionally have been included as part of the benefits package for college employees. Specific holidays and their number vary among institutions, usually based on the academic calendar. Most such calendars provide Christmas Day, New Year's Day, the Fourth of July, Labor Day, Memorial Day, and Thanksgiving Day as paid holidays, with the total number ranging approximately from six to twelve. The costs of holidays can be reduced if they are designated during periods when classes are not in session.

Holiday policies typically include certain eligibility criteria; the following statement is an example. "Employees will be entitled to pay for college holidays, provided they are in pay status (that is, receiving remuneration from the college through working, sick leave, vacation, or funeral leave) on the workday immediately preceding the holiday and the workday immediately following the holiday." Such eligibility criteria tend to reduce absenteeism, which can become excessive immediately preceding or following a holiday.

Sometimes a policy statement is included that requires an individual to have been employed at least 30 days prior to the holiday in order to receive holiday pay. Another form of controlling holiday pay cost relates to eligibility for holidays subsequent to resignation. The following is a typical policy statement: "If an employee terminates employment, he or she will not receive pay for holidays occurring after the last day worked, even though the holidays fall within the period of projected terminal vacation leave."

Most institutions provide some form of premium pay for employees who are required to work on a college holiday. This may range from providing pay for the time worked, plus pay or equivalent time off for the holiday, to double time for all hours worked on a holiday in addition to the holiday pay (triple pay). Regardless of the type of premium pay offered, it should be stated carefully in writing so that it is understood by everyone involved.

Another policy consideration is the calculation of overtime for a pay period that includes a holiday. Some employers compute weekly overtime on the basis of time worked rather than time paid. Other employers calculate overtime on the basis of time paid, which could include holidays, vacation, sick leave, and funeral leave. Regardless of the options selected, a clear policy statement is desirable.

A sample policy, which incorporates holiday time as a basis for weekly overtime compensation, might state: "Any college holiday for which the employee receives pay will be counted as a day worked for computing weekly overtime, unless a holiday falls on an employee's regular day off, when he or she will be given one day's pay at the regular straight time rate. In such case, the unworked holiday shall not be included as hours worked for the purpose of computing overtime." Since it is possible that an employee could receive both premium pay and overtime pay for the same hours, it is quite common for a policy statement to include a disclaimer for the payment of both, such as, "Whenever premium pay and overtime pay are both applicable, only the overtime pay will be paid."

There has been a trend to prorate holiday pay for part-time and temporary employees. When these employees are granted holiday pay, the eligibility criteria are usually more stringent than those for regular, full-time employees. Such a policy is illustrated as follows: "Payment for college holidays will be prorated dependent on the part-time employee's regular weekly work schedule, provided: (1) the employee has been on the staff at least 30 days immediately preceding the holiday, and (2) the employee works the last college workday preceding the holiday and the first college workday following the holiday."

Vacations

Although vacation allotments vary among employers, there are standard allocations to serve as a basis for policy development. Two weeks of paid vacation are common for nonexempt employees and three weeks are typical for middle managers. Four weeks are standard for exempt or administrative employees. It is also usual for employers to increase paid vacation for nonexempt employees, based on their length of service with the institution. This allowance is frequently increased to three weeks of vacation after five or more years of service and four weeks after ten or more years of service as tangible recognition and appreciation.

Some caveats should be considered in drafting vacation policies. Vacation should generally not be given in advance, that is, employees should be required to earn vacation by working a specified period before being eligible to use vacation. A typical policy is to stipulate that vacation earned in one year (or shorter period) is to be used in the next year (or shorter period). For example, "vacation will begin to be earned on employment, but will not be available for use until the beginning of the month following six months of employment." The policy should also clearly state whether employees earn vacation based on their anniversary date or within a fiscal year and should address the carryover of vacation from year to year. For example, "The vacation year is July 1 to June 30. All vacation earned in a vacation year must be used by June 30 of the following year." The absence of such a control could impair a department's ability to operate efficiently.

The policy should contain a statement that vacations are to be scheduled in advance and at a time agreeable to the employee's supervisor in accord with the needs of the department. Holidays that occur during an employee's vacation are not usually charged against the employee's vacation balance. The policy should also state whether extra pay in lieu of vacation is permissible or prohibited. There may be unusual instances where such pay is allowed, but generally it should be discouraged.

The policy should state the minimum and maximum amounts of vacation that can be used at one time, for example, "vacation may not be taken for less than one day, nor for more than two weeks." In instances where a vacation preference must be decided between or among employees, seniority or length of service is an excellent determinant.

Finally, the policy statement should include a specific statement regarding how much time an employee must work during a designated period in order to earn vacation. A sample follows: "Employees will earn vacation at their appropriate earning rate provided they are in a 'pay status' for at least 15 workdays during the calendar month, or at one-half of their appropriate earning rate provided they are in a pay status for at least 10 workdays, but less than 15 in the month." Vacation balances should be centrally maintained in the personnel or payroll office.

A few employers stipulate that an employee forfeits vacation benefits on discharge, or on failure to give two weeks' notice on resignation. However, the legality of these provisions is questionable and they should not be used without the advice of legal counsel.

Sick Leave

It is traditional to grant employees some protection against loss of pay because of illness or injury that is not related to occupation (worker's compensation covers accidents occurring on the job). Sick leave programs that afford employees paid time off based on hours worked are common to the majority of colleges. The sick leave earning base varies but generally ranges from one-half day per month to one day per month. Some colleges place restrictions on the total amount of sick leave accumulation. Some offer their sick leave programs as the sole income protection for illness or accidents of employees; others coordinate sick leave with either short-term or long-term disability insurance programs. (These programs are described in the "Insured Benefits" section of this chapter.)

Most institutions have historically viewed sick leave programs as "insurance" type programs, that is, programs to be used in the event of illness or accident; however, some colleges have modified their programs in recent years. The standard modification provides a form of payout, usually at a reduced rate, for sick leave that has been earned but not used. The payout does not usually become operable until the employee has accumulated sick leave to a certain level. These modified programs are usually intended to curb sick leave abuse. Each institution must decide the advantages and disadvantages of such an approach. A more common reward for employees who do not use available sick leave is to provide a lump sum payment at retirement equivalent to the accumulated balance, or to a percentage of the accumulated balance.

Despite these reward systems, sick leave abuse has become widespread. Measures such as written warnings and disciplinary suspensions may be required to check such abuse. Various considerations should be included in sick leave policy statements. For example, the earning rate should be clearly stated as well as the smallest unit, if any, in which sick leave may be used. Employers that permit sick leave to be used in units as small as one hour or less may find significant abuse, such as employees leaving work early. Limiting sick leave to units of not less than four hours usually controls such abuse. However, there are obvious disadvantages to minimum use requirements, and each institution should weigh such options carefully.

A policy statement should indicate that sick leave is to be used only for the *employee's* illness, unless a more liberal use is desired. It should also state whether sick leave can be used for medical and dental appointments. To control abuse, some employers require a licensed physician to verify the illness.

It is also common to base approval of sick leave on the "timely" notification by the employee of his or her supervisor. This is usually established as a certain time prior to the beginning of the scheduled work shift or within one hour after the beginning of the shift. A sick leave policy should also provide for continuing notification by an employee during an extended illness. Sick leave benefits should be made available for all types of illness as a matter of good personnel practice. Employers, by law, must not exclude temporary disabilities relating to pregnancy from provisions of a sick leave program.

Colleges should stipulate in the written policy how much time an employee must work during a designated period in order to earn sick leave. This eligibility criterion is usually the same for both vacation and sick leave.

Personal Leave

A relatively new policy among colleges is to provide employees with paid personal leave ranging from one to three days per year. Personal leave is usually intended to cover one-day absences which occur occasionally for business or personal reasons or for religious holidays. Employers usually require advance notice and supervisory approval for absences, but generally supervisors are advised to accommodate employees' "personal leave" requests whenever possible. Many college administrators believe that the existence of a personal leave policy permits them greater control of vacation requests and schedules. However, adequate reporting and approval controls should be made a part of such policies.

Funeral Leave or Bereavement Leave

Most colleges provide funeral leave with pay to employees following the death of a member of the immediate family or other relative. Institutions differ in the number of days accorded employees, the definition of immediate family and other relatives, and the purpose of the leave. Many problems can be avoided by having the policy distributed in writing to the campus community. An example follows: "Funeral leave of three work days with pay will be granted immediately following the death of a member of the immediate family or household. (Immediate family is defined as husband, wife, father, mother, son, daughter, brother, sister, father-in-law, mother-in-law, daughter-in-law, son-in-law, stepfather, stepmother, stepson, or stepdaughter.) One additional funeral leave day will be granted for funeral services for a member of the immediate family that are conducted beyond a 300-mile radius of the college. Funeral leave of one workday with pay will be granted for the funeral of the following relatives: grandfather, grandmother, grandchild, brother-in-law, sister-in-law, uncle, aunt, nephew, or niece."

Although most policy statements will not be this detailed, they should be sufficiently inclusive to permit consistent interpretation and administration. Many institutions provide one day off with pay, but on request will permit additional unpaid time off. Other institutions charge funeral leave against an employee's sick leave balance.

Jury Duty and Court Witness

Colleges often provide leave for jury duty without loss of pay. Some institutions compensate the employee based on the difference between his or her regular pay and the amount received for serving as a juror. A few institutions have expanded the jury duty provision to include service as a court witness in cases where the employee is not a party. Submission of a subpoena prior to such duty is usually a condition of compensation.

Declared University Closings

Many institutions have developed compensation policies to cover declared university closings for inclement weather, days of mourning, acts of God, etc. It is advisable to develop a policy in advance to cover unusual situations. Generally, such closings occur on short notice and do not provide sufficient time to develop reasonable compensation policies for the occasion.

An example of a compensation policy for a declared college closing follows: "This sets forth the compensation policy for certain college holidays or closings, which shall be only as declared by the board of directors or the president of the college and shall include declared days of mourning and days set aside to honor a specified person or event. The policy is applicable to unique, one-time closings that are generally of not more than one day's duration.

"Permanent, part-time, and temporary employees who are scheduled to work, or who are in a pay status but do not work due to the closing of the college for the reasons indicated, will be paid according to the hours they were scheduled to work that day. (In other words, they will not suffer a loss in pay due to the closing.) Employees who are not scheduled to work, those who are on a scheduled day off, or on temporary or permanent layoff will not receive compensation.

"Employees who are required to work to maintain essential or necessary services on the declared day will receive their regular rate of pay for the hours normally worked plus a comparable amount of pay or equivalent time off computed at their regular hourly rate for the hours worked. An employee will be considered to have worked or have been scheduled to work on the declared day if the majority of his or her regularly scheduled shift falls on the declared day.

"This policy excludes closing or reductions in work force related to college vacation periods, energy or resource shortages, or other conditions beyond college control. (Such closing or reductions in work force shall be considered temporary or permanent layoffs, as appropriate.)"

Leaves of Absence

Colleges usually have either written or oral policies covering leaves of absence for staff employees. Such policies typically accord the employee continuity of employment and service credit for the period of the leave. Leaves of absence usually are granted without pay for periods not to exceed six months for purposes such as education, military service, personal reasons, family emergency, child care, or maternity. Maternity leaves, by law, must be of the same duration as other leaves and *may* be with pay, that is, the employee can be eligible to use sick leave for a period of temporary disability, as determined by a physician.

A college should have a written policy for leaves of absence. Many such policies use a specific length-of-service condition as an eligibility requirement, for example: "Generally, leaves of absence are not granted unless the employee has five or more years of service at the college."

Leaves of absence policies usually permit the employee to continue insurance benefits during the leave and to return to the same job at its expiration. In some instances, if the college continues its share of the premium cost for insurance benefits during the leave, an employee will be required to reimburse the college for these premium costs if he or she fails to return to work for a period of time equal to the leave of absence. Another condition may base continuation of the institution's share of the premium on the type of leave taken. Many colleges also permit individual supervisors to authorize informal leaves of absence without pay for up to two weeks. Requests for leaves of absence should be made in writing and approval should be granted in writing. (See Exhibit 3B.)

Any eligibility or contingency requirements for leaves of absence should be explained to employees in a general policy statement, as in this illustration: "In determining eligibility for leaves of absence without pay in excess of two weeks, the college will review the supervisor's recommendation, the employee's work record, the employee's length of service, leave previously granted, and the reason the leave is being requested. If granted, a leave of absence guarantees the employee the right to return to the same or similar job at the expiration of the leave. All leaves will be calculated from the last day of actual work. An employee may be paid vacation as of the beginning date of the leave (last day of work), but this does not extend the period of the actual leave. An employee's seniority continues to accrue during a leave of absence; however, vacation and sick leave are not accumulated during a leave of absence. If an employee fails to return at the expiration of the leave for at least the period of time comparable to the period of the leave, he or she will be required to repay the portion of the insurance premiums paid by the college during the leave of absence. Whenever the circumstances under which a leave is granted are altered, the leave is immediately cancelled and the employee must return to work." Some policies also state that failure to return at the expiration of the leave is tantamount to resignation.

Educational Assistance Plans

Most colleges have developed liberal "educational assistance" programs for staff employees, in which tuition is reduced or waived. This benefit should be well publicized to employees and to prospective employees since it can serve as an excellent recruitment, retention, and development tool for the institution. Usually such programs offer reduced or waived fees for courses that are (1) related to the employee's present job, (2) related to the employee's potential development within the college, or (3) part of a program leading to a degree as determined from an approved plan of study.

Frequently, such plans require one year of service with the institution as a condition for program eligibility. Most educational assistance programs incorporate limitations on the types and number of classes that may be taken during the employee's workday. Usually, an employee will be allowed one class during work hours, provided that the class is directly related to improving the employee's job performance and is not offered at times outside the employee's work hours.

In addition to these standard tuition waiver programs, some colleges extend similar educational benefits to dependents of employees. Some institutions further sweeten the educational benefits for employees' dependents by paying part or all of their tuition at another college. Usually, the college limits its tuition contribution to a specified amount.

Ancillary Benefits

There are many other noninsured benefits offered by institutions of higher education that should be reduced to writing and communicated to employees. Examples of such programs are:

Discounts on athletic and concert tickets
Discounts at college bookstores
Health center privileges
Library privileges
Recreation privileges
Blood banks
Uniforms
Check cashing

Insured Benefits

Programs described in this section typify insured benefits, in which a college contracts with an insurance carrier to provide certain coverages.

The cost of various insurance programs, particularly health insurance, has risen dramatically during the last few years, and the trend continues. Therefore, prudent management requires continual review, monitoring, and comparison of cost, coverages, and claims to insure cost-effective and competitive insurance programs.

Contributory vs. Noncontributory

Whether the college should share premium costs for insurance programs with employees—or to what level these costs should be shared—is a subject of controversy. Insurance carriers and employers traditionally have adhered to the belief that more effective claims control results when employees share the premium costs. However, the current trend is for employers to absorb an ever-increasing share of the premium costs of various insurance programs because of a growing need to offer benefits that are competitive. Unions have persuaded many employers to agree to noncontributory programs and this trend has subsequently crept into the nonunion environment. Noncontributory coverage today typifies, to a greater degree, life insurance programs, and to a lesser degree health insurance programs and long-term disability programs. Short-term disability programs are frequently noncontributory.

Mandatory vs. Voluntary Enrollment

In noncontributory programs, enrollment is usually mandatory. In contributory programs, however, where the employee is required to share part of the premium cost, mandatory enrollments can provoke strong objections. An employer can usually justify the mandatory enrollment program if the employee pays the lesser share of the premium.

Mandatory enrollment occurs primarily as a requirement of insurance carriers that stipulate participation of a high percentage of the eligible group as a contract condition. Carriers believe they can reduce the possibilities of "adverse selection," that is, that only employees with health problems will enroll, by having an enrollment requirement.

Health Insurance

Health insurance programs cover doctor and related medical practitioner care, hospital and related medical facilities use, and prescription drugs. The two primary types of health insurance plans are: (1) *basic hospital-surgical-medical insurance*, and (2) *major medical insurance*.

Basic Hospital-Surgical-Medical Insurance. The well-known Blue Cross-Blue Shield plans are representative of typical basic health insurance programs. Many other carriers offer comparable plans. Generally, these plans provide a "schedule of benefits" that outline the basic coverages and sometimes the exclusions of the plan. New employees are usually covered from the first day of employment, but there may be a waiting period or a period of open enrollment, such as a specified month each year.

Carriers of "basic" health insurance generally offer a series of benefit schedules from which the employer selects the level of coverage desired. The "usual and reasonable" or "usual and customary" schedule is generally the most expensive because it provides for total payment or full reimbursement of covered expenses. These "usual and customary" schedules are updated periodically by carriers in order to keep pace with rising costs.

In addition to the full reimbursement coverage described above, most carriers offer at least two other schedules that provide for payment or reimbursement of expenses based on limited days of hospital coverage, and have a dollar ceiling for schedules. Although basic health plans may provide essentially the same coverages and indemnification schedules, the premium costs can differ considerably among them because of a group's claims experience or the carrier's cost of operations.

Following are suggestions for efficient cost-control measures in basic health insurance:

1. Program costs can be reduced significantly by *not* providing first dollar indemnification or reimbursement coverage; and by coordinating the basic program with a major medical plan (see page 113). The contract should include a "coordination of benefits" provision whereby claims are coordinated and shared with other group plans under which an employee may be covered.

2. The employer's premium contribution can be limited to the employee only and not applied to dependents. It should be kept in mind, however, that there are considerations other than cost associated with this option.

3. Faculty, staff, and spouses who reach age 65 should be transferred to Medicare and Medicaid supplements. Most programs offer high and low supplements that provide benefits similar to basic health insurance programs at considerably reduced costs. Under Department of Labor regulations, health benefits by a Medicare supplement must be equal to those provided by an employee benefit program. If the institution's basic health plan is experience-rated, separate claims experience should be

requested for Medicare supplements, if both these plans are with the same carrier.[4]

4. Claims experience reports and occurrences should be analyzed to determine adverse claims experience and areas where coverage should be reduced or expanded. An attempt should be made to negotiate rate increases with the carrier, and to project the cost impact of proposed changes in the level and types of benefits.

5. If coverage of prescription drugs or dental or optical coverage is offered, it should be included in the major medical plan rather than in the basic plan to reduce initial dollar coverage and premium costs.

6. Take advantage of "pooling" rates, whereby adverse claims above a certain level are shared with other employers.

Major Medical Insurance. Most colleges follow a two-plan approach to health insurance, that is, a basic hospital, surgical, and medical plan coordinated with a major medical expense plan. As the name implies, major medical plans were designed to indemnify employees against catastrophic medical expenses. It is not unusual for plans to have expense ceilings of $100,000 to $250,000 or higher. A recent trend in major medical program design has been the limitation of the deductible, a feature that limits an employee's total out-of-pocket expenses to a specified amount, usually one thousand or two thousand dollars in a calendar year. Most major medical plans reimburse 80% of covered expenses that are not reimbursed in the basic plan.

If institutions place most benefit plan improvements in their major medical plan, premium cost impact will be smaller than if more benefits are contained in the basic plan.

Several major medical plans incorporate dental insurance as an option. Such plans usually cover, at the level of 80% or lower, certain dental expenses that exceed $500 or $1000. Colleges that are contemplating dental coverage should explore limited coverage under the major medical plan in order to control costs.

Most plans are calendar-year plans, that is, all covered expenses incurred during the calendar year are combined for purposes of computing the deductible. A feature of many plans is the "family" deductible, which provides for reimbursement based on a deductible of $100 per individual or $300 per family.

---

[4]NOTE: Responsibility for enforcement of the Age Discrimination in Employment Act, as amended, was transferred from the Department of Labor to the Equal Employment Opportunity Commission (EEOC) effective July 1, 1979. The Department of Labor had promulgated regulations concerning employee benefits under the Act prior to the transfer. However, EEOC announced after the transfer that it would conduct its own analysis of the Act's effect on employee benefits and then issue guidelines on the subject. As of this writing, EEOC has not yet revealed its guidelines.

Major medical plans are a necessity in health insurance programming; the catastrophic illness or accident must be indemnified or personal financial disaster could result.

Health Maintenance Organizations. In the last few years, the preventive medicine concept has become popular, and Health Maintenance Organizations (HMOs) have emerged to provide prepaid, comprehensive medical service, which is offered for a flat premium without regard to indemnification schedules. Federal regulations govern an employer's responsibilities with respect to HMOs; these regulations, which include determination of the employer contribution, may be found in NACUBO's *Federal Regulations and the Employment Practices of Colleges and Universities.*

Disability Insurance

Over the last decade, employers have taken major strides to protect their employees against loss of income because of illness or accident. Disability insurance programs have evolved as a primary vehicle which provides income continuation during periods of disability. There are two primary types of disability insurance: short-term disability plans and long-term disability plans.

Short-Term Disability Plans. The traditional form of short-term assistance at colleges is sick leave. An increasing number of colleges are replacing or coordinating their traditional, noninsured sick leave program with an insured short-term plan. Employers have moved to coordinated plans primarily to stabilize and limit their potential costs. Such plans usually provide income replacement at approximately two-thirds of salary for disabilities occurring from either accident or sickness. Typically, these plans have a one- to two-week waiting period and a total benefit period of either 13 weeks or 26 weeks. (On-the-job injuries, which are covered under worker's compensation, are generally excluded from coverage.)

Short-term disability plans provide income continuance for periods of temporary disability. If employees are disabled for five months or longer, they may be eligible for social security disability payments. Short-term disability plans offer excellent protection and security to employees; however, their cost is high. Disability contracts should include a provision that disabilities be verified by a licensed physician and not by the carrier's claims administration personnel. This provides for a more objective determination and one which ultimately will receive greater acceptance by employees.

Long-Term Disability Plans. Long-term disability (LTD) plans are far more common than short-term plans in higher education. The customary dividing line between short- and long-term plans is the initial six-month period. Few disabilities extend beyond six months and many colleges provide sick leave for part or all of the first six months of disability. Long-term disability plans frequently are provided to exempt employees only; insurance carriers are reluctant to extend such coverage to nonexempt employees. The benefits from such plans are frequently reduced, offset by, or coordinated with disability payments from social security and other benefit plans, thus reducing direct costs of the LTD plan.

LTD plans generally have two periods and definitions of disability. The first period is usually for two years; disability is determined by a licensed physician, and is defined as inability to perform the regular duties of one's occupation. The second period, which typically commences after two years or 24 months, defines disability as total incapacity, as determined by a licensed physician, to perform the duties of *each* and *every* occupation for which one is qualified by reason of training, education, or experience. As with the short-term plans, exclusions are generally made for occupationally related injuries or diseases, which would be covered by worker's compensation. Pregnancy, which had been a common exclusion from LTD plans, is now included because of the Pregnancy Discrimination Act requirements. LTD plans offer the ultimate in income continuance during prolonged periods of disability.

Life Insurance

Many colleges offer group term life insurance for faculty and staff (contributory plans typically require an enrollment of 75% or 80% of the eligible group as a contract condition). Individual coverage is either a flat amount or an amount based on a percentage of salary. A common practice is to offer coverage of from one to two times annual salary. Plans based on salary provide increased insurance coverage along with increases in salary.

Another feature in life insurance programming is supplemental life insurance, whereby employees may opt for variable additional coverage in specified amounts or increments of annual salary. In addition, employees may purchase insurance for dependents in flat amounts, such as $5,000. This optional insurance is usually fully paid by the employee through payroll deduction. Most group life plans incorporate accidental death and dismemberment (AD&D) coverage as part of the base plan or as a supplement. This feature, which is relatively inexpensive, provides specified indemnification for death resulting from accident or for dismemberment of certain parts of the body.

Maintaining coverage for retirees is a sensitive concern for institutions. Many insurance contracts have no provision for retiree life insurance; others reduce the face amount of coverage by 50% at retirement and some reduce the level to a nominal amount, such as $5,000. An institution that fails to reduce significantly the face value of coverage for a retiree will ultimately be confronted with staggering claims experience and significantly higher premiums.

Most plans incorporate a "waiver of premium" provision, that is, premiums are automatically waived for an employee who becomes "totally and permanently" disabled. If this feature is not included as part of a plan it can be added at very little cost.

Miscellaneous Insurance Coverages

Accidental death benefits may be provided by a blanket insurance policy covering employees while off the campus but traveling on college business. The cost of "airport insurance" or personal accident insurance policies should not be a reimbursable travel expense if a college insurance policy of this type is in effect.

Colleges should also be alert to the "dread disease" insurance programs that provide insurance for cancer, diabetes, etc. The coverages are very specific and usually are not justified in terms of the premiums paid and the probabilities of occurrence. Employees who desire such coverage can obtain it directly from the carrier.

In addition to typical health, life, and disability insurance programs, carriers have developed "mass merchandising," which is not a true group program, for automobile and homeowners insurance. These programs usually do not include any premium contributions from the employer. However, employers are responsible for payroll deductions of premiums. The premium costs for the employees are purportedly discounted for group participation. These programs have received mixed reviews from institutions that have made them available to their employees because of the risk that any dissatisfaction with claims handling or costs will reflect on the college. Institutions should carefully review and analyze the experiences of other employers who have tried these services.

Retirement Programs

The retirement program probably represents the single largest benefit investment for any college. A well-designed retirement plan is essential for the attraction and retention of a qualified faculty and staff. In designing retirement plans, institutions must consider income options, portability, vesting requirements, whether the plan will be contributory or noncontributory, whether it will be based on defined benefits or defined contributions, whether it will be self-administered, and a host of other factors. Retirement programs must be administered in accordance with provisions of the Employee Retirement Income and Security Act of 1974 (ERISA).

Retirement plans fall into two basic categories: (1) defined benefit plans, in which the payout for the employee at retirement is fixed by formula and (2) defined contribution plans, in which the amount paid into the plan is fixed and the payout is variable.

Defined Benefit Plans

Under a defined benefit plan, retirement income is fixed as so many dollars per years of service or as a percentage of salary in the last years or highest salary years prior to retirement. To be adequately funded, these plans require that funds be set aside in advance which will allow, by actuarial assumptions, for the uncertainties of salaries, life expectancies, investment earnings, and projected years of service.

Defined Contribution Plans

Under the defined contribution plan, the fixed factor is the periodic payment into the fund on behalf of the employee. The retirement payment or annuity will depend on investment earnings and life expectancy. TIAA-CREF plans are defined contribution plans.

Most college retirement plans are contributory, that is, the college and the employee share in the contributions. The majority of retirement programs are mandatory, usually after one or two years of service. Variables to be considered in designing a retirement plan are complex; institutions should thus consult experts before establishing programs or modifying existing programs.

Preretirement Planning Programs

While most colleges have retirement programs, most have failed to provide planning, counseling, or programming for the transition into retirement. However, in the last several years, institutions have recognized this serious void in their benefit programs and have taken steps to correct it.

Preretirement planning programs are offered on many campuses to assist employees to prepare for retirement. Such programs are designed to provide prospective retirees information on the multiple facets of retirement. Former retirees, doctors, lawyers, accountants, and recreational enthusiasts are used as faculty to aid prospective retirees in the transition; programs are generally offered on a voluntary basis and their costs are nominal. (A recent book on the subject by Ronald Garrison and Clark England entitled *Retirement—A Time For Fulfillment*, published by CUPA, provides a thorough description of preretirement planning.)

Statutory Programs

Small colleges can realistically consider the option to self-insure some statutory benefit programs, including those that follow.

Worker's Compensation

Injuries arising out of or during the course of employment are covered under state worker's compensation laws. Although such laws vary from state to state, they have many similarities. In most states, employers may self-insure for worker's compensation; however, some states prohibit this practice. Under worker's compensation laws, employers are held responsible for the reasonable medical care and expenses of an injured employee as well as for continuing compensation as specified by indemnity schedules for specific periods of time. Most state laws also require compensation for permanent-partial and permanent-total disabilities as well as for death resulting from injury. Since campus employment historically has been nonhazardous, college employees suffer few disabling injuries. Because of the limited exposure to risk, many colleges self-insure their liability under worker's compensation laws.

Some institutions negotiate a form of coinsurance with a private carrier under which the college becomes totally liable for any expenses up to $10,000. The insurance carrier assumes liability for expenses in excess of the $10,000 ceiling per injury. This type of coinsurance is an effective hedge against catastrophic claims, yet it significantly reduces premium costs to the institution. Some colleges purchase comprehensive worker's compensation insurance; this truly reassigns the risk to the insurance carrier, but the premiums for such coverage can be expensive.

Unemployment Compensation

General guidelines for unemployment compensation are prescribed for the states by federal laws. Each state, in turn, has its own law which complements the federal law. These laws vary somewhat among states, but generally the differences relate primarily to compensation amounts and eligibility periods. Under federal law, colleges have the unique option of determining whether they wish to pay the unemployment tax rate on their eligible payroll or be billed for actual charges under the "reimbursement" method. The tax option is comparable to insurance because the employer is limited to the maximum tax rate regardless of the number of claims against the organization. Very few colleges have selected the tax method, because the unemployment compensation costs usually are much less under the reimbursement method. Several small colleges have found it cost-effective to retain consulting firms, which specialize in unemployment compensation administration.

Colleges should have an organized review process for unemployment compensation claims. An apathetic approach to claims review can be costly to the institution.

The following practices can help to minimize unemployment compensation claims:

1. Maintenance of detailed records of the reasons for separations. This includes file documentation of the circumstances, carefully worded for all separations, that is, resignations, discharges, etc. Supervisors responsible for termination notices should be apprised of the need for carefully worded statements.

2. Possible use of contract services or temporary help to avoid frequent layoffs in areas of fluctuating or intermittent employment patterns.

3. Careful review of probationary employees and early separation of those who are unsatisfactory.

4. Appointment of one person to be responsible for knowledge of the college's policies and procedures.

5. Vigorous pursuit of appeals and reviews; use of consultants or legal counsel for assistance in preparing claims, appeals, and reviews.

Under federal law, faculty members are ineligible to draw unemployment compensation between terms and during summers if they have a contract for the subsequent term. The office responsible for personnel records is probably in the best position to administer an effective "notice of claim" review and to file a timely response as required by law.

Social Security

Social security is the basic social welfare program in the United States. The benefits from social security are substantial and provide financial assistance not only in retirement but for unforeseen contingencies as well, such as disability and death. Social security taxes have risen dramatically in recent years (in 1980 the taxable wage base became $25,900, with a rate of 6.13% for both employees and employers), but so have the benefits, which are pegged to the cost of living.

Exhibit 3A$_1$ **Total Projected Compensation Analysis Sheet**
                   For _____

Department _____

Salary

(annual equivalent based on 40 hours per week) $ _____

Retirement

(10% of one's annual equivalent wage)   _____

Social Security

(6.05% of wages)   _____

Blue Cross

(provides basic hospital coverage)   _____

Major Medical

(after basic medical coverage, reimbursement is
made for 80% of the covered expenses up to
$25,000 and 100% from $25,000 to $250,000
after a deductible)   _____

Life Insurance

(provides two times one's annual wage
equivalent)   _____

Disability (long term)

(provides 50% of one's wage beginning with the
seventh month of disability)   _____

Financial Aid

(tuition assistance for one's children at this
college)   _____

                              Total Compensation $ _____

Based on the above data, your fringe benefit package represents_____
percent of your annual equivalent wage.

Exhibit 3A$_2$

Employee's Statement of Personal Benefits (1)						
(Staff Benefits and Participation in Other University Sponsored Programs)						
Equivalent Annual Salary	Retirement Contribution	Social Security	Group Life Insurance	Accidental Death-Dismem.	Total Disability	Comprehensive Medical
$	$	$	$	$	$	$
	Workmen's Compensation	Tuition (2) Scholarship	Annual Paid (2) Holidays	Annual Paid (2) Vacation	Annual (2) Sick Leave	Travel Accident Insurance Coverage
			*	*	*	*
	$	$				

(1) In Addition to Annual Cash Salary (2) Other University Sponsored Programs	Total Compensation	Personnel benefits paid by this college represent _____ percent of your equivalent annual salary or wages. This does not include programs marked with an asterisk (*).

Exhibit 3B

LEAVE REQUEST FORM

SOCIAL SECURITY NUMBER ⎢ ⎢ ⎢ ⎢ ⎢ — ⎢ ⎢ — ⎢ ⎢ ⎢ ⎢ ⎢

NAME · DEPARTMENT · DATE

PAID LEAVE — Reason for Absence (Mark "X" in Appropriate Box) — UNPAID LEAVE

| a | COMPENSATORY TIME OFF (CTO) | b | JURY DUTY (J.D.) | c | PERSONAL LEAVE (PL) | d | SICK LEAVE (SL) | h | EXCUSED ABSENCE (EA) | i | UNEXCUSED ABSENCE (UA) |

| e | SICK LEAVE POOL (SLP) | f | OTHER PAID (OP) | g | VACATION (V) | W | Bereavement (B) | j | OTHER UNPAID (OU) | k | SICK LEAVE/UNPAID (SLU) |

REQUESTED LEAVE PERIOD AND PAY STATUS

Instructions: Place an "X" in the box for each **work day** of the month in which you were or will be absent. Indicate the number of **work days** absent with pay and those with no pay in the designated space.

MONTH: ___ DAY OF MONTH ___ COMMENTS

| 1 | 2 | 3 | 4 | 5 | 6 | 7 | 8 | 9 | 10 | 11 | 12 | 13 | 14 | 15 | 16 | 17 | 18 | 19 | 20 | 21 | 22 | 23 | 24 | 25 | 26 | 27 | 28 | 29 | 30 | 31 |

MONTH: ___ DAY OF MONTH

| 1 | 2 | 3 | 4 | 5 | 6 | 7 | 8 | 9 | 10 | 11 | 12 | 13 | 14 | 15 | 16 | 17 | 18 | 19 | 20 | 21 | 22 | 23 | 24 | 25 | 26 | 27 | 28 | 29 | 30 | 31 |

Number of days with pay _____ . Number of days with no pay _____ .

DISTRIBUTION:
WHITE: PERSONNEL   CANARY: EMPLOYEE
PERS. 141-577 REV. (6-77)

EMPLOYEE'S SIGNATURE · DATE

SUPERVISOR · DATE · DIR. OF PERS. · DATE (PERSONAL LEAVE ONLY)

4. training & development

Colleges and universities historically have been labor-intensive, investing up to 70% or 80% of operating budgets in human resources. Ironically, administrators in higher education have been dilatory in recognizing that the development of human resources, as well as the creation of an organizational climate conducive to development, directly relates to attainment of institutional mission and goals. Training and development should pervade the organization.

Management should prepare staff to be receptive to change. Rapid technological advances may cause obsolescence, and this can render staff and institution incapable of responding to the students. In most colleges and universities, training and development have been dealt with only on an ad hoc basis. If training continues to be viewed from such a narrow perspective, as a relief for occasional ills, it will be perpetually relegated to a low-priority status. An attitude that encourages development is necessary if training is to flourish.

Training Programs

Training and development on college campuses range from nothing more than informal, on-the-job training to formalized, comprehensive, multipurpose programs covering all classes of employees. The breadth and scope of a program appear to be directly related to institutional size, administrative commitment, and program budget.

Some colleges and universities have developed excellent training programs at minimal cost by using existing resources, such as talent available on the campus. Basic programs can be developed at little cost. Examples of available resources include expertise of faculty members, short courses organized by the extension or continuing education division, training sessions by telephone and office machine companies, adult education courses at local high schools or community colleges, and training programs through local chambers of commerce and various industrial associations.

There are two essential components in any effective training and development program, regardless of scope: first, careful identification and specification of training needs and second, definition of objectives designed to meet identified needs.

Identification of Needs

Identification of training needs, or "needs assessment," generally concerns two areas: institutional and individual. Institutional needs are most often identified through development of a survey instrument circulated among administrators. The administrator identifies training programs that should be made available to improve employee skills and abilities and, ultimately, job performance.

Because training and development programs have not been widely used for staff employees in higher education, it is possible that supervisors and administrators are themselves unaware of the kinds of programs that are most needed. Therefore, the survey instrument should list a series of basic training programs that could be offered. Each supervisor should select programs that would be most beneficial to employees in his or her unit. In addition, the instrument should be designed to solicit ideas for other programs that the supervisor believes would benefit the unit. Basic programs could include skills development programs such as typing, shorthand, letter writing, and data entry; apprenticeship programs; supervisory training; sensitivity training; and time management.

Supervisors should be directed to review their employees' job descriptions, performance appraisals, and, if they exist, departmental goals and objectives. Specific employee problems that could be corrected with training programs should also be listed on the survey instrument.

Individual training needs can be determined from reference to various sources, including employees, who have specific knowledge on the subject. Employees should be encouraged to review their job descriptions and performance appraisals and the departmental objectives in identifying training needs.

Use of a survey instrument is time-saving and efficient, and has the advantage of demonstrating management's interest in assisting employee development. Once the surveys have been completed, the "wants" must be culled from the real "needs," and priorities should be established on the basis of greatest need and available resources.

Training and Development Objectives

Training objectives should be expressed in simple, pragmatic terms that have common meaning to supervisors and employees. The training program should be designed to affect what is frequently referred to as "terminal behavior," that is, to improve performance or performance potential. The objectives should describe the skills and behavior that are expected to result. They should explain what the training will do, how it will benefit an employee, how it will help the employee to better perform a job, and how it will prepare him or her to do other, related jobs. The processes for identifying needs and defining training objectives have necessarily been abbreviated in this book, but the principles are essential to a sound program.

For a training and development program to be successful, college administrators must determine the principles of the program. They must know what the program is intended to accomplish, as well as the procedures that will best facilitate these objectives. Such objectives should be developed both for single training activities and for a series of training programs.

Institutions should begin such programs slowly and gradually develop their quality. This approach has been successful; it can also facilitate requests for additional programs. (See Exhibit 4A).

Employee Orientation

Employee orientation is one of the foremost basic training programs in use today. Unfortunately, many employers tend to devote such programs primarily to signing insurance papers. However, comprehensive orientation programs can be designed for minimal cost and can acquaint new employees with their environment, work rules, benefits, and pertinent policies and procedures. Such programs can set the stage for a positive and lasting employment relationship, reducing the turnover of new employees by integrating them into the work force.

Since colleges and universities generally recruit new staff employees from business and industry, an orientation program should present the unique features of higher education. Programs can be easily modified to accommodate one or two employees.

While the information conveyed in orientation programs may not be fully retained, these programs have the residual benefit of demonstrating the institution's interest in the new employee. They also afford the college an excellent opportunity to communicate the spirit of the institution. Orientation programs should provide the new employee with reference material, such as booklets describing policies and benefits, which can be read later at the employee's leisure. New employees come to a job with high expectations of doing well, and the institution should encourage this attitude. (See Exhibit 4B.)

Elements of a Training Program

Three basic elements must be considered in any training the institution offers:

1. *Timetable and Organization of Material.* This is essential. How

much skill is the employee expected to acquire in what period of time? Both the timetable and the program should be explained so that the employee comprehends the purpose and benefits of the training. Frequency of instruction should be predetermined. Instruction material, training location, and equipment should be prepared in advance.

2. *Presentation.* Learning usually is best acquired through multiple modes of presentation. The program should be explained and illustrated by those presenting the program and then, preferably, performed by the employees being trained. Studies conducted by the Western Electric Company in the late 1920s revealed that 90% of a person's job performance development was the result of experiences in performing rather than of formal classroom learning.[5] Instruction should be clear, concise, and complete.

3. *Follow-Up and Evaluation.* Follow-up and evaluation are essential in determining the progress of the trainee as well as the quality of the program. Although imperfect, evaluation remains the best means for assessing the trainee's knowledge and deficiencies; it also provides valuable information with which to improve techniques and programs.

Types of Training Programs

On-the-job training (OJT). This is the form most commonly used in higher education. However, OJT is frequently approached on an informal basis with little concern for, or application of, sound training principles or techniques. Supervisors frequently assign training responsibilities to the most senior employee in a unit because this person knows the operation best. While possession of job knowledge is important in training, the ability to instruct or to impart knowledge is equally so. On-the-job training can be more efficient if proper training techniques are integrated into the program. Job rotation is a variation of OJT that is frequently used and is a relatively inexpensive method of developing employees' skills and knowledge.

Vestibule training. This is a term applied to programs that simulate job conditions. Such training is especially useful for training large numbers of employees in a relatively short period of time, where acquisition of a few skills is the primary objective. The "role playing" technique is a widely used form of vestibule training.

---

[5]Studies conducted by the Committee on Work in Industry of the National Research Council at the Hawthorne (Chicago) Works of the Western Electric Company.

Programmed Learning. In this method, information is imparted with the aid of a machine. Material to be learned is projected on a frame, followed by a question or problem related to that information. The trainee selects an answer; if it is correct, a new frame of information is projected on the machine. If the response is wrong, the original frame is repeated.

This process continues until the trainee masters the framed information. Programmed learning or instruction is very useful as an individual training aid, and can be purchased from a number of sources at a relatively modest cost.

Internship programs. These have grown in popularity as a training medium; they usually begin with a period of textbook instruction, followed by a form of on-the-job training in which acquired skills are nurtured in the work setting. Such programs combine theory and practice, permitting the intern to apply what has been learned. They are an excellent means by which employees can be apprenticed to higher-level jobs. College libraries are an example of a major area in which internship programs can be used.

College Courses. Some colleges use regular or specially designed courses taught by their faculty as a form of employee training. The cost of instruction is reduced because of the availability of this resource. Tuition and fee waiver programs are not only a popular employee benefit, but also serve as a developmental tool and a useful employee recruitment aid.

Apprentice Programs. These are another popular training approach for developing skilled crafts, trades, and technical personnel. Many colleges have been forced to develop such programs because of the institution's inability to pay prevailing craft and trade rates. Apprentice programs typically provide for a minimum of two years and a maximum of six years of apprenticeship. They offer unskilled employees an excellent career ladder. Such programs combine textbook instruction and on-the-job experience under the instruction of a journey-level worker. (See Exhibit 4C.)

Performance Appraisal

Performance appraisal is one of the more controversial practices in personnel administration. The controversy turns not on disagreement as to whether performance should be evaluated, but rather on such basic factors as how and when an appraisal should be communicated to an employee. The "ideal" performance appraisal form has yet to be developed. Misgivings about performance appraisal are heightened because supervisors are often apprehensive about appraisal interviews—the communication of appraisal results to the employee.

Nevertheless, performance appraisal should be an integral part of any personnel program. The positive aspects of performance appraisal far outweigh the negative. Such evaluation can provide both the institution and the employee with various benefits, such as those indicated in the objectives of performance appraisal listed below:

1. Above all, to let employees know how well they are performing their jobs.

2. To improve employee performance through counseling, which can motivate individual development.

3. To provide employees deserved recognition.

4. To identify additional training needs.

5. To justify salary increases, transfers, and promotions.

6. To assist employees in their personal and professional development.

7. To help employees realize their maximum potential in their jobs.

Performance appraisal results have also been used in determining the order of layoffs and sometimes as documentation for disciplinary action. A supervisor should use the appraisal process to gain a better understanding of the employees' potential and to develop and train employees for maximum use of their abilities. From the employees' perspective, the process demonstrates how well they are progressing and in what ways they can improve.

The performance appraisal process should stimulate job interest, because it formally recognizes efficient performance as well as unsatisfactory performance. Once employees have satisfactorily completed a probationary period, performance appraisals should be conducted on an annual basis, usually on the employee's anniversary date or on a fixed date for all employees.

Performance Standards

A supervisor's most important responsibility is to manage effectively the human resources he or she is assigned. Effective management entails meaningful communication between the supervisor and the employee. Nowhere in the supervisor-employee relationship is communication more important than in establishing performance standards. The supervisor, at the onset of the employment relationship, should communicate to the employee what is expected and what will be measured or evaluated. The position description should serve as the basic document in setting standards. This description should be succinct and accurate, and describe what the job requires. Sometimes it is necessary to augment the description to establish meaningful standards. Only by following this basic step can performance standards be established that are jointly understood by the employee and the supervisor.

Conducting Performance Appraisal

To be truly fair and effective, a performance appraisal program should provide instruction to supervisors on performance appraisal terms, hazards, and techniques. The limited availability of training personnel makes this difficult to achieve in a small college. If the training cannot be given, performance appraisal forms should include detailed instructions and definitions of rating terms. Following are important considerations:

1. The form should stress that each factor to be rated should be examined separately. Supervisors should not be influenced by their overall opinion of the employee's performance, but should consider only the employee's performance that relates to the factor being rated.

2. Supervisors should be cautioned against permitting one or two recent or unusual incidents to influence their judgment; their evaluation should be made on regular, day-to-day performance.

3. The evaluation should be reflective of the entire appraisal period. If the appraisal period is for one year, the supervisor's evaluation should be for that length of time.

4. The length of service should not be an influencing factor, except where it is germaine to the employee's work.

5. The evaluation should generally reflect only the supervisor's judgment of the employee's performance, not the opinions of others.

Most colleges and universities employ graphic rating scale forms for performance appraisal; these use terms such as "outstanding," "superior," "average," etc. Unfortunately, these terms mean different things to different people and thus should not be used, if possible. Many forms provide definitions of terms and the factors to be evaluated. (See Exhibits $4D_1$ and $4D_2$.)

Evaluation of an employee's performance should be conducted by the employee's immediate supervisor, who typically assigns and checks work and is ultimately accountable for it. In order to insure consistency in ratings, some colleges require the supervisor's superior to review and sign the employee's performance appraisal. This encourages the immediate supervisor to conduct an honest and objective appraisal of the employee's performance, and can also improve communication between the two supervisors.

The performance appraisal document should be a multicopy form, usually of at least three copies; the original should be kept in the central personnel files. A second copy should be retained in the department or area of the employee's assignment, so that the supervisor can use it as a tool for counseling. The third copy is given to the employee.

Performance Appraisal During Probationary Period

Performance appraisals should be conducted frequently during the probationary period. For example, at least two appraisals should be conducted in a period of three months. The primary purpose of performance appraisals during the probationary period is to eliminate substandard performers. By conducting more than one appraisal during this period, a new employee can be apprised of deficiencies that may be corrected prior to the expiration of probation.

The probationary period should be viewed as an extension of the selection process. Communication between the supervisor and the new employee through performance appraisal should assist the employee in adapting to the new work environment and in gradually assuming a full work load.

The Appraisal Interview

The appraisal interview is essential to performance appraisal; without it, the program is incomplete and incapable of effectively improving job performance. One *cannot* improve an employee's performance by completing an appraisal form. One *may* improve an employee's performance by offering helpful suggestions and adequate instruction and guidance through the appraisal interview.

Supervisors often approach appraisal interviews with apprehension, particularly if the appraisal reveals areas of unsatisfactory performance. It is important to deal with this feeling, because more harm than good can result from an appraisal interview that is improperly conducted. Prior to conducting the appraisal interview, the supervisor should carefully plan what he or she will say and how it will be said.

An appraisal interview should be held in a private setting that is free from interruption and conducive to candid communication. Adequate time should be reserved for the interview and it should be scheduled when neither the supervisor nor the employee is under great pressure. Prior to the interview, the supervisor should review pertinent material, including previous appraisals, and determine what he or she wishes to accomplish during the interview. The appraisal form should serve as the basic document of the appraisal interview. The supervisor should review in detail the performance standards and the ratings assigned the employee and plan specific suggestions for improving the employee's performance.

The employee should be encouraged to state his or her point of view. The supervisor should anticipate the employee's reaction to the subjects to be discussed, and have an opening statement well prepared. It is good practice to begin the interview by praising the positive aspects of the employee's performance. Areas where improvements are required should next be discussed, with specific suggestions on how improvement might be achieved. The interview should be concluded by summarizing the positive aspects of performance, as well as the suggested methods for improving performance. (See Exhibit 4E).

Appraisal Pitfalls

Certain pitfalls in performance appraisal can affect the validity of the process. The five most common are:

Halo Effect. Supervisors may rate all traits or factors the same as one trait or factor because they are favorably or unfavorably impressed by performance concerning the one factor. For example, if an employee has a good attitude, the supervisor may overlook shortcomings of his or her performance.

Severity Tendency. A rater may be overly critical of performance because he or she has established unrealistic or unachievable performance standards. This can produce a "What's the use?" reaction from employees.

Leniency Tendency. A rater may be overly generous and rate all employees high on all factors, even though some may not have earned the high rating. This is unfair to employees and removes their incentive to improve performance.

Central Tendency. A supervisor may rate all employees within a narrow range, usually toward the middle; he or she may be dishonest because of a fear of being candid. This often misleads and confuses employees.

Recency Error. A rater may base a rating on what is most easily remembered, that is, the most recent behavior of the employee may decide the rating. Instead, the rater should consider the most typical behavior of the employee over an entire appraisal period.

Though performance appraisal is clearly a subjective process, it can be effective only where it is administered as objectively as possible. If a supervisor has erred in a rating and this fact comes to light during the appraisal interview, the supervisor should be honest and change the rating accordingly. On the other hand, the supervisor should not be "bullied" into altering a rating that he or she believes to be accurate. Objectivity and consistency are the keys to fair performance appraisal.

Factors and Traits to Be Evaluated

Factors on which employees will be evaluated should be selected with utmost care. Generally, "personality" traits should not be used. If administrators insist on the inclusion of such traits, they should be kept to a minimum. A performance appraisal form should be designed to evaluate only the employee's job performance. If personality characteristics relate to job performance, which is sometimes the case, they should be handled by individual comments from the supervisor.

Some researchers have suggested that performance appraisals should be limited to quality of work, quantity of work, and interpersonal relations. However, most appraisal forms measure from six to nine factors: (1) quality of work, (2) quantity of work, (3) job knowledge, (4) organization of work, (5) dependability, (6) attendance and punctuality, (7) human relations, (8) attitude and cooperation, and (9) initiative.

The ultimate selection of performance appraisal factors should depend on the relation they have to the job. There are three criteria an appraisal trait or factor should meet:

1. Can it be perceived? Can the rater reasonably observe the trait?

2. Is it uniform? Is the trait a common and an important characteristic of all jobs to be rated?

3. Is it distinctive? Can the rater clearly distinguish this trait from others being evaluated?

If these three qualifications are met, the trait should probably be included on the performance appraisal form.

Validity of Performance Appraisals

Performance appraisals have a higher validity when they are based on actual performance factors and not on personality traits. Further, when performance appraisals correlate directly to salary increases, their validity decreases. Apparently, supervisors tend to be less honest in their appraisals of employee performance if that appraisal is the sole factor in determining an immediate salary increase. A supervisor may not wish to deny a low-paid clerk a merit increase and thus may inflate the performance appraisal. To use performance appraisals fairly as determinants for merit salary increases, an appraisal should be conducted three to four months prior to the scheduled effective date of an increase.

How To Determine Training Needs

The following article was prepared by John A. Dombroski, of the Pennsylvania State University, for the "How-to" series published by the College and University Personnel Association.

Employees of the present day have many aspirations, expectations, and needs that differ from those of previous generations. These new employees are interested, curious, and involved; they want to know "why."

An excellent way to satisfy these needs and desires and to provide employee motivation is through training programs. The need to train and upgrade personnel exists in every college or university work area. This article provides guidelines for determining training needs, a first step in an effective training program. Although it is primarily directed toward service and clerical personnel, the principles described also apply to technical and semiprofessional personnel.

An effective training program requires more than a positive attitude on the part of senior management. It is essential that one person be given the responsibility for coordinating efforts to plan the program, administer it, and see that enthusiasm is continuous; this responsibility cannot be dispersed among the supervisors and other managers involved, although their wholehearted cooperation is necessary to success.

Determining Actual Needs

If each employee's capabilities are to be utilized to the utmost, training must be based on *actual* needs, rather than on *supposed* needs. Some sources for determining what training needs really are, in any area of operation, include:

1. *Personal observation.* Many examples of inefficiency or waste are evident through observation, such as the practice of making extra, unnecessary copies of documents, or using two cups of detergent for a cleaning job when only one is specified.

2. *Discussions with employees and supervisors.* The person performing a job and the supervisor overseeing the job are the experts on any operation. Seek their thoughts regarding training needs; a questionnaire may be helpful.

3. *Maintenance records.* Not every department keeps maintenance records, but it does pay bills or process transfers of funds. It is not difficult to determine whether any maintenance expenses are recurring; if they are, and this is caused by human failure, training may correct the problem.

4. *Production records.* Departments are often lax in keeping production records; in some cases, keeping such records requires too much time to be worthwhile. However, information on production is available from supervisors, either in written or oral form, and covers items such as number of rooms cleaned, time spent making beds or distributing linens, time required for the preparation of salads, or time to collate papers for distribution.

5. *Job descriptions.* These can be reviewed to determine whether certain tasks are being performed poorly; this can indicate training needs.

6. *Merit ratings.* Every supervisor evaluates employees, either formally or informally. A review of such evaluation can indicate specific employees who would benefit from training, and may also indicate work areas in which training is needed.

7. *Discussions with students and student employees.* In many operations of a college or university, students and student employees are very close to the work areas and understand some of the problems. Their ideas may be helpful.

8. *Cost records.* Check cost records; ideas for cost reduction can be found. Training may help with this.

9. *Accident reports.* If supervisors investigate accidents to determine their causes, training needs will often become evident.

10. *Training committees.* Such committees, composed of supervisors or of supervisors and employees (either institution-wide or departmental), may be able to identify training needs and work closely with the person responsible for training program coordination.

11. *Exit interviews.* Discussions with employees leaving their jobs may identify needs for training that could help to reduce turnover.

12. *Personnel records.* A review of these may pinpoint areas where training has been lacking in quality or quantity.

13. *Complaints and grievances.* These may identify areas where a lack of understanding exists, and often are indicative of the need for certain training programs.

14. *Employee attitudes.* Poor employee attitudes may be related to poor supervision and point to the need for supervisory training.

Exhibit 4B

How to Orient New Employees

The following article was prepared by Donald C. Zick, of the University of Missouri, for the "How-to" series published by the College and University Personnel Association.

There are many purposes behind the orientation of new employees, most of which fit well under two major headings:
1. To provide valuable, standardized information.
2. To help develop attitudes that will enable new employees to get off to a good start.

Phases of Orientation

Orientation programs are typically accomplished in three phases:
1. Employment office briefing.
2. Centralized formal sessions.
3. On-the-job orientation by the individual's supervisor.

Employment Office Briefing

Employment interviewers should explain:
1. Salary.
2. When, where, and to whom the new employee reports.
3. Job duties and responsibilities.
4. General activities of the department in which the new employee will serve.
5. Schedule of benefits.
6. General information on housing and transportation.

Formal Centralized Sessions

Formal, centralized orientation programs vary widely in length and type. Usually coordinated by the training section, these sessions should be the heart of any orientation process. A *sample* agenda of a typical, well-organized, centralized approach follows:

8:00 a.m. *Introduction*
1. Program purposes
2. Preview of the program
3. Introductions

8:10 a.m. *Welcoming Address*
1. Presented by a high ranking college or university officer.
2. It is suggested that the officer cover:
   a. The important part the college or university plays in its service to the local community, state, and nation.
   b. Traditions that will lead employees to be interested in the organization.
   c. Personal feelings of the officer concerning why the institution is a good place to work.
   d. Future prospects of the college or university.
   e. Why each individual should become an above-average employee.
   f. Other "pep talk" subjects that will develop pride in the institution as a place to begin a lifetime occupation.

8:30 a.m. *Film, Slide Series, etc. on the College or University*
1. Origins of the institution.
2. All campuses (if more than one).
3. Available fields of educational specialization.
4. People and services that provide and support the student programs.
5. Responsibilities of the institution.
6. Tour of the buildings and grounds.

9:00 a.m. *Educational Opportunities*
1. A description of available employee educational programs, and those yet to be developed.

9:30 a.m. *Coffee Break*

9:45 a.m. *Personnel Policies and Noninsured Benefits*
1. Pay
2. Working hours
3. Overtime
4. Rest periods
5. Holidays
6. Vacations
7. Worker's compensation
8. Leaves
9. Promotions and transfers
10. Jury duty
11. Work schedules
12. Attendance
13. Employee organizations
14. Grievance procedures
15. Sick leave
16. Others

11:00 a.m. *Insured Benefits*
       1. Medical insurance
       2. Life insurance
       3. Retirement program
       4. Others
11:45 a.m. *Summary and Question and Answer Period*
12 noon   *Adjournment*

In most cases, information covered in such an agenda does not lend itself to the decentralized approach. The supervisor has a part, but should not be required to explain all this.

The person responsible for presenting these sessions should be notified at specified intervals (every two weeks or a month) of new employees hired, their addresses, and their supervisor's name and address. After a certain number of employees have been hired, a session should be organized, and the employees scheduled, by letter, to attend. Necessary clearances for this program must be obtained prior to sending out letters for a session.

On-The-Job Orientation

To insure that supervisors know their on-the-job orientation responsibilities, each should be given an orientation checklist.

Such a list might contain:

1. Tour of department
   a. Introduction to fellow workers.
   b. Explanation of activities and operations, including a tour of the building or plant and a description of the organization.
   c. Location of wash rooms, cafeteria, bulletin boards, bid sheet boards, etc.
2. General Information
   a. Parking.
   b. Transportation.
   c. Where and how to enter the premises.
   d. Starting and quitting times, lunch periods, shifts, etc.
   e. Rate of pay and increases, including when, where, and how paid.
   f. Overtime—probability, methods, rates, etc.
   g. Advancement—lines of promotion, bidding, and how to prepare for promotion.
   h. Safety policy—reporting and avoiding accidents and where to obtain medical attention.

    i. Local rules, such as smoking, rest periods, and use of the telephone.

    j. When and whom to call in case of sickness.

    k. Good student contact principles.

3. Work assignment
   a. Arrange for first work assignment.
   b. Provide the necessary training to do the job.
   c. Designate person to whom to go for help.
   d. Explain how to obtain the necessary tools and supplies.
   e. Check on work performance.

4. Coaching
   a. Discuss with the employee how well he or she is doing.
   b. Discuss the employee's adjustment regarding work and work group.

Each new employee typically comes to employment ready to do a good job. During this early period he or she forms important attitudes and develops a standard concerning quality and quantity of work. It is important that needed information is effectively provided to create positive attitudes.

Exhibit 4C

How to Start an Apprentice Program

The following article was prepared by William L. Hetrick, of the Pennsylvania State University, and Arthur F. Lindberg, of Brown University, for the "How to" series published by the College and University Personnel Assocation.

A carefully planned and well-executed apprentice program in a college or university can be a useful source of skilled workers. Such a program also may provide opportunities for members of minority groups to become proficient in skilled and technical fields.

Applicability

In its strictest sense, an apprentice program is possible only in the "skilled trades." It is a structured program of specified length, usually 6,000–8,000 hours, designed to train an individual to become a skilled worker in a craft or trade. State apprenticeship councils and the Department of Labor's Bureau of Apprenticeship and Training provide certain standards to which a program must adhere before a qualified apprentice may "graduate" with Department of Labor certification. Some of the trades for which apprentices may be trained are:

Air Conditioning Mechanic	Meat Cutter
Automotive Mechanic	Machinist
Carpenter	Maintenance Mechanic
Electrician	Painter
Electronic Technician	Plumber
Glassblower	Sheetmetal Mechanic
Baker	Steamfitter
Cook	

This is by no means a complete list. The final determination of which trades may properly have apprentice programs rests with the Bureau of Apprenticeship and Training.

Determination of Need

The fact that a college or university employs, or expects to employ, workers in a given trade does not necessarily mean that an apprentice program is indicated. The department supervisor must be ready to assume the responsibility for training a beginner and to have experienced workers spend time in instructing apprentices. Therefore, it is imperative that willing and able supervisory personnel are available before initiating an apprentice program. The next step is to determine how many apprentices can be accommodated. The Department of Labor has certain guidelines to assist in this matter.

A primary concern may be the department budget and how many apprenticeships it will permit. Also, planning for the absorption of the apprentices into the college or university work force, after completion of their program, must be carefully considered. As a rule of thumb, a desirable ratio is five skilled workers to one apprentice; however, this is only a guideline, and obviously it must give way when there are fewer than five and a training need is apparent.

Program Structure

An initial and difficult job is planning the apprentice program, which includes two segments—related training and on-the-job work processes. The related training usually consists of a specified number of hours of home study and classroom sessions, covering job-related subject matter, both practical and theoretical. The work processes portion consists of structured "packages" of hours that include the basic duties and responsibilities comprising the total job. These processes become the training format for the supervisor to follow in the day-to-day development of the apprentice, insuring that all segments have been covered when the apprenticeship is completed.

Finally, there should be effective and regular follow-up on both segments of the program. This includes accurate recording of grades received on all "book work" and monthly reports of progress on the work processes, together with performance ratings of the apprentice. These records should be retained in a central location.

Program Development

Apprentice programs can be developed independently or in conjunction with the Bureau of Apprenticeship and Training. However, if there is an organized bargaining unit in an area in which apprentice training is contemplated, it is essential that the union's cooperation and approval be enlisted. Certification by the U.S. Department of Labor cannot be attained without such approval.

A vital contact to make is the state or area apprenticeship council, a body that coordinates and approves apprentice programs in a given locale. (In some states the burden of consulting and coordinating is left by default to the National Bureau of Apprenticeship and Training.) These agencies have model apprenticeship agreements that indicate the ways various unions or companies have organized their programs. Available models can be adapted to individual situations. A complete wage schedule also must be developed and made a part of the formal agreement. The Bureau can assist with this matter, although, if the institution is unionized, the rate must be negotiated with union representatives. An apprenticeship council can also outline steps that lead to the setting up of an approved apprenticeship program, from the drafting of the agreement and standards to state and federal certification.

The concurrence of both the union and the apprenticeship council in an institution's apprentice program count heavily in its favor, but this does not necessarily guarantee approval by state and federal authorities. If one or more of the craft unions represented on an apprenticeship council questions the adequacy of the program's apprenticeship standards, it may be difficult to win approval. The backing of the appropriate union should be obtained prior to submitting a program.

Exhibit 4D₁

Performance Appraisal

PITFALLS IN COMPLETING A PERFORMANCE APPRAISAL

Pitfalls

1. *The Isolated Incident*

   A rating should not be based on a few isolated performance incidents. When this is done, the rating is unfairly influenced by nontypical instances of favorable or unfavorable performances.

2. *The "Halo" Effect*

   The "Halo" effect occurs when one factor influences ratings on all factors.

   Examples: An employee's work is of good quality, therefore, other ratings (such as those on promptness or work quantity) are higher than normal. Another employee is frequently absent, with the result that the ratings on other factors are unusually low.

3. *The "Cluster" Tendency*

   The tendency to consider everyone in the work group as above average, average, or below average. Some raters are considered "tough" because they normally "cluster" their people at a low level. Others are too lenient. "Clustering" overall ratings usually indicates that the rater has not sufficiently discriminated between high and low levels of performance.

Suggestions

1. Consider the entire appraisal period. Try to enumerate high points and low points in performance, then assign a rating that typifies the individual's normal performance.

   Do not attempt to assign a rating to an element of performance and then create justification to support it.

   Be able to explain the reason for each rating.

2. Rate each factor independently.

   When rating more than one person simultaneously, it may be helpful to rate all employees' performance on one factor rather than one employee's performance on all factors.

   Use the overall rating to give weight to individual factors.

3. In a group of people in similar jobs, performance is likely to be spread over most performance categories.

   Review your own record as a rater. Check the tendency to be either "too tough" or "too lenient" in your appraisals.

4. *Rating the Job and Not the Individual*

   Individuals in higher-rated jobs are often considered superior performers to those in lower-rated jobs. This normally means that confusion exists between the performance appraisal and how the job has been evaluated.

4. Consider how an individual is performing in relation to what is expected.

   Rate the person's performance, not importance of the job.

5. *Length of Service Bias*

   There is a tendency to allow the period of an individual's employment to influence the rating. Normally, performance levels should be higher as an individual gains training and experience, but this is not always the case.

5. Recognize that some people may never achieve top ratings, regardless of length of service.

   Watch closely the progress of newcomers and be ready to recognize superior performance if it is achieved.

PERFORMANCE AND WORK APPRAISAL FORM

Date_____19____ Annual_____ _____ Probationary_____
Name_____
Job Title _____ Department _____
How long under your supervision _____ Employment Date _____
Judge the employee on the basis of the work now being done. Be sure that each characteristic is considered separately, regardless of where the appraisal falls on any of the other characteristics. Place a check (X) in front of the phrase that best describes the individual. The space under each characteristic is provided for additional comments.

1. Quality of Work

   _____Careful Worker. Works quickly. Checks Work. Thorough and neat.

   _____Work is reasonably complete, accurate and presentable.

   _____Quality occasionally unsatisfactory. Must be checked for errors.

   _____Work usually lacking in thoroughness, accuracy or neatness.

Additional Comments: _____

Strengths: _____

Areas for Improvement: _____

2. Quantity of Work   _____Very fast, does exceptional volume of work.

_____Produces amount of work expected.

_____Produces less than normal volume as compared with others in same work.

_____Amount of work entirely inadequate.

Additional Comments: _____

Strengths: _____

Areas for Improvement: _____

3. Knowledge of Facets   _____Thorough knowledge of job requirements
   of Job   and department. Can work independently
                                      and handle new situations.

_____Good working knowledge of own job.

_____Limited knowledge. Not completely aware of functions of job; needs additional training.

Additional Comments: _____

Strengths: _____

Areas for Improvement: _____

4. Attitude Towards Job   _____Puts in extra time when needed, helps others.

_____Acceptable interest and enthusiasm.

_____Wastes time and does personal things during working hours.

_____Needs prodding; shows no interest and disturbs others.

Additional Comments: _____

Strengths: _____

Areas for Improvement: _____

5. Contacts   _____Cheerful, courteous, and tactful.
   (Personal & Telephone)   _____Can usually handle situations requiring tact, courtesy and cheerfulness.

_____Often offends people.

_____Not Applicable.

Additional Comments: _____

Strengths: _____

Areas for Improvement: _____

6. Cooperation

_____Exceptionally successful in working with and assisting others.

_____Generally works well with and assists others.

_____Difficult to get along with. Does not cooperate well.

_____Fails to cooperate. Unwilling to work with or assist others.

Additional Comments: _____

Strengths: _____

Areas for Improvement: _____

7. Reliability

_____Can always be trusted with confidential information and money, and to safeguard property and equipment.

_____Exercises normal care in safeguards.

_____Undependable. Needs constant supervision. Frequent errors in judgment.

Additional Comments: _____

Strengths: _____

Areas for Improvement: _____

8. Initiative

_____Initiates and makes suggestions for improvements in work procedures. Interest and ability to think alone.

_____Keen interest and enthusiasm toward work.

_____Does needed jobs without being asked to do so.

_____Does very little without being instructed.

Additional Comments: _____

Strengths: _____

Areas for Improvement: _____

9. Attendance

_____Excellent Record

_____Good attendance record. Rarely late or absent without calling.

_____Often fails to conform to work hours.

_____Excessive amount of unexcused absences.

Additional Comments: _____

Strengths: _____

Areas for Improvement: _____

GENERAL COMMENTS

1. What suggestions do you have for furthering this employee's advancement?
   a. What additional on-the-job training would be helpful?
   b. What evening school subjects would assist the employee in making progress?
   c. What other suggestions do you have?
2. In what area can this employee make improvement?
3. Has there been an overall improvement since the last evaluation?
4. Please note below any additional information which has not already been covered.

Date of review with employee_____

Employee's signature _____

Review made by:_____

Approved by: _____

THE APPRAISAL INTERVIEW

A. *Preparation*
   1. Review the performance and work appraisal form.
   2. Have examples ready.
   3. Allow adequate time for the interview.
   4. Permit no interruptions.
   5. Plan what to say.
   6. Plan how to say it.
B. *The Interview*
   1. Put the employee at ease.
   2. Allow the employee to talk at least 50% of the time.
      Some listening responses are:
      a. Silence
      b. Nod
      c. Casual comment
      d. Echo
      e. Reflective summary
   3. Be sure to listen to what is said.
   4. Be prepared for disagreement.
   5. Have a helpful attitude and build on the person's strengths.
   6. Discuss specifics—not generalities.
      a. Avoid universal criticism
      b. Do not dwell on personality
   7. Talk about the employee—not you.
   8. Read between the lines.
   9. Do not become emotionally involved.
      a. Empathize
      b. Understand the employee's point of view
   10. Find out what else is on the employee's mind.
   11. Avoid:
      a. Direct comparison with other employees
      b. Arguing
      c. Soft pedaling major weaknesses
      d. Negative approach to weaknesses
      e. Forcing your ideas on the employee

Exhibit 4D$_2$

Performance Evaluation

Any employee, whether full-time or part-time, is entitled to a periodic review of his or her work with his or her supervisor. A very important function of the supervisor is to convey to employees how well they are doing in their work and what changes or improvements are expected.

The following appraisal procedure helps to provide the answers to two basic questions that are of concern to all of us.

1. How well am I doing?
2. Where do I go from here?

Formal performance evaluation at many colleges is something relatively new. It is not intended to provide answers to all of the performance-related questions that occur in a work situation. It is, however, intended to efficiently address three basic principles.

1. To record and communicate the capacities and accomplishments of an employee during a given period.
2. To assist in determining merit increases and future promotions.
3. To assist employees in planning future objectives and realistic steps for personal growth and development within the college.

Attached is a formal performance evaluation form to be used in evaluating all staff members in your organization. The form is designed to be straightforward and easy to use. It provides (9) universal traits, with (5) ratings ranging from outstanding to inadequate. This performance evaluation tool and approach is intended to lend objectivity to your evaluations. Before conducting your evaluations, the following basic rules should be read and applied:

1. Be sure an up-to-date job description is available. This description should be read to be sure you understand the exact responsibilities of the job. Without so doing, you may be expecting more or less than the job requires or the employee understands. If the duties being performed differ from the description, the personnel services office should be contacted for a job review.
2. Performance review should be conducted at least every (6) months, but not less than once each year. The current review should be compared with previous ones to measure performance change. Reviews should not be made under time constraints and should be made far ahead of the annual budget recommendations. Last minute evaluations may result in unfair and incomplete recollections.
3. Jobs and incumbents of the same title should be evaluated together for comparative purposes, e.g., clerks compared to clerks, secretary I's to secretary I's, accountant II's to accountant II's, program directors to program directors, etc. Since the duties and responsibilities of each different classification vary, it would be unfair and misleading to compare them against each other; only like jobs should be compared. If no like jobs exist in your organization, performance should be compared against the established job description and mutually agreed-on performance expectations.
4. If no job description exists for this job, contact the personnel services office to receive assistance in preparing one.
5. In applying the results of the evaluations for purposes of merit increase distribution, a number of approaches can be used ranging from a ranking of high to low, to more sophisticated analytical approaches. Regardless of the approach, one basic principle should apply: In a given population, a few people will receive above average and below average increases. The majority will receive an average increase.

    The ranking approach can be applied as follows:
    A. For each of the (5) quality ratings, the lowest rating of inadequate would be (1) point, increasing by (1) point for each factor up to (5) points for outstanding.
    B. Within each classification, rate each employee, using their total point accumulation as a basis for ranking.
    C. Using the principle cited above, the budget/merit resources available to you and the distribution of points, categorize the salary increases into above average, average, below average.
6. A thorough and unrushed appraisal interview should occur between the evaluator and the employee. The objective of these interviews should be for both parties to communicate with each other regarding the job, the work, the performance evaluation, and future goals and objectives relative to performance, and the employee's immediate and future career.

7. Management by objectives is an increasingly popular and effective management style. This approach sets forth some specifically enumerated performance or production goals and timetables. It clearly documents what is to be accomplished in the future and provides an obvious standard on which to base future evaluations. The last page of the evaluation provides a space for enumerating mutually agreed upon performance or production objectives. These objectives should also include specific goals for the employee's personal growth and job development.

A sample list of objectives might be as follows:

Performance and Personal Development Objectives
19XX/XX

John Doe, Accountant I   Supervisor, J. J. Kidd
February 1, 19XX

Objectives   Time Table
a. Initiate billing forms within (5) days   July 1, 19XX
b. Attend supervisory seminar   September 1, 19XX
c. Complete course in managerial accounting   January 1, 19XX
d. Empty incoming work basket by end of day   February 1, 19XX
e. Become thoroughly familiar with affirmative action goals   Immediately

8. Relative to flow or distribution of evaluation forms, budget instructions, preparation time, etc., this information should be available from each department head. General information relative to performance evaluation, employee counseling, job classifications, pay plans, etc., is available from the personnel services office.

Name	
Division/Department	Budget Number
Position Classification	Position Number

Time in Position	Years	Months	Date of Last Performance Evaluation	Date of This Evaluation

NOTE: Before initiating this review, a job description should be available for review. This review should be conducted on the basis of the requirements set forth in the job description proposed for this position.

QUALITY RATINGS

		Needs	Fully Meets	Exceeds		(Must be accompanied by detailed comments or examples)
1. Inadequate	2. Improvement	3. Requirements	4. Requirements	5. Outstanding		

	Check One					COMMENTS
	1	2	3	4	5	
1. QUALITY OF WORK (extent to which work is done well)						
2. QUANTITY OF WORK (amount completed on time)						
3. DEPENDABILITY (attendance, punctuality, loyalty— Will the job get done in the manner it should?)						
4. JOB KNOWLEDGE (the amount of knowledge one has about the present job)						

	Check One					COMMENTS
	1	2	3	4	5	

5. INITIATIVE
   (acting on own responsibility in carrying out assignments, learning more about the job, etc.)

6. ABILITY TO RELATE OR INTERACT WITH OTHERS
   (How well are assignments which involve others accomplished, including matters of a sensitive nature?)

7. CONTRIBUTIONS TO AFFIRMATIVE ACTION
   (decisions or actions that have resulted in resolution of underutilization of women and ethnic minorities.)

8. SUPERVISION AND TRAINING OF OTHER STAFF
   (If applicable)—The accomplishment of work assignments and through the work performance of subordinates reaching desired objective. Also, helping staff members supervised to acquire work related skills, knowledge and experience.

9. PROMOTIONAL POTENTIAL AND APTITUDE DISPLAYED FOR GREATER RESPONSIBILITY

Describe staff member's outstanding accomplishment(s) since last review.

Recommendations for continuing development and improvement

NOTE: Before conducting an appraisal interview with the employee, the job description should be read by both the supervisor and the employee and it should be used as the reference for discussion about work performance.

STAFF MEMBER'S COMMENTS	Who Last Evaluated Your Performance?	
	When Were You Last Evaluated?	Were you given an opportunity to discuss the evaluation? ☐ Yes ☐ No

STAFF MEMBER'S COMMENTS

Who Last Evaluated Your Performance?

When Were You Last Evaluated?

Were you given an opportunity to discuss the evaluation?   ☐ Yes   ☐ No

For me to improve my work performance or qualifications for promotion, I feel I need:
   (e.g., skill training—"hands on" experience, closer supervision, college courses, etc.)

Please List

Other Comments

Employee's Signature

PERFORMANCE AND PERSONAL DEVELOPMENT OBJECTIVES

List objectives and time commitments for each to which the staff member and supervisor mutually agree.

OBJECTIVES	TIME TABLE
[add space as needed]	

Staff Member's Signature | Date

Supervisor's Signature | Date

Exhibit 4E

How to Conduct a Performance Appraisal Interview

The following article was prepared by Wayne P. Strong, of the California Institute of Technology, for the "How-to" series published by the College and University Personnel Association.

An appraisal interview should help improve an employee's job performance by:

1. Informing the employee of his or her overall performance rating and of the criteria used in determining the rating.

2. Providing open discussion on how the employee can correct any weaknesses and build on strengths.

3. Clarifying any misunderstandings about the job and what is expected of the employee.

4. Building a stronger relationship between the supervisor and the employee.

Preparation for the Interview

More harm than good can result if the appraisal interview is improperly conducted. Therefore, careful planning is necessary prior to conducting the interview. The supervisor should:

1. Schedule an appointment that allows sufficient time, when neither the supervisor nor the employee is under great pressure.

2. Provide for privacy; keep interruptions to a minimum.

3. Review pertinent background information, including personnel records, performance and project status reports, and job descriptions.

4. Decide what is to be accomplished in the interview. This requires having clearly in mind the performance criteria used, then carefully measuring the reasons for giving a specific rating, and determining what improvement is needed or is possible.

5. Consider the employee's point of view. Anticipate what his or her reaction to the discussion might be, remembering that each employee is different and each may react differently in an interview.

6. Have an opening statement carefully prepared, in order to begin the discussion satisfactorily.

7. Be in a good frame of mind. If the supervisor is upset or angry, the interview should be delayed to a more appropriate time.

8. Have the necessary forms or information ready to present at the proper time; searching for such information during an interview is distracting.

Beginning of the Interview

The supervisor's introductory remarks often set the tone of the entire interview. It is to everyone's advantage to create a friendly, constructive atmosphere at the outset. The supervisor should:

1. Be natural. The approach should be friendly, courteous, and businesslike.

2. Put the employee at ease and establish rapport. This can be done by a pleasant greeting and a friendly statement that is of interest to the employee and requires a reply.

3. Explain the purpose of the interview and how the employee was appraised. The employee should have a clear understanding of the criteria used in determining the rating.

Discussion of the Appraisal

This is the crux of the process. The supervisor should be ready to face various reactions from the employee. Most employees are doing a satisfactory job and are happy to know where they stand and how they can improve. However, dealing with employees who are not doing a good job or who are skeptical of the ratings is more difficult. The following guidelines may be useful in dealing with either situation. The supervisor should:

1. Compliment the employee without going to extremes. Failure to recognize good performance may cause a "What's-the-use?" attitude. However, overdoing the compliments will raise questions about one's sincerity and supervisory ability.

2. Make criticism constructive. If pointing out a weakness, offer a means to correct it.

3. Clarify the reasons why the rating was given, citing specific examples of performance. Deal with facts and avoid generalities.

4. Be sure the employee knows what is expected of him or her. The employee may be confused and not realize that expectations are not being met.

5. Ask questions and then listen. Allow the employee to express reactions to the evaluation; this can result in discovering the underlying causes for marginal performance.

6. Don't interrupt—but make sure the discussion is not side-tracked by irrelevant topics.

7. Ask the employee for suggestions on how job performance can be improved. Use this opportunity to guide employees in such improvement.

8. Keep the appraisal job-centered. Avoid discussion of personality shortcomings unless they adversely affect departmental operations or the employee's performance.

9. Try to maintain objectivity; don't show anger or hostility, regardless of any hostile remarks the employee may make.

10. If the employee gets angry, listen. Don't expect to convince the employee of anything while he or she is angry.

11. Allow the employee self-respect. Nothing is gained by "proving" the employee wrong, being sarcastic, overbearing, or unduly stern.

12. Develop and obtain the employee's commitment on specific steps for improvement and any follow-up activity. This should be written down, if necessary.

Closing the Interview

1. Summarize the discussion and plans for improvement.
2. Schedule a follow-up interview, if necessary.
3. End the interview on a friendly, constructive note.

After the Interview

The supervisor should consider the following questions. If it is possible to answer "yes" to each of them, the appraisal interview has been successful.

• Does the employee clearly understand his or her position in regard to the job?

• Does the employee clearly understand the reason for any unsatisfactory rating?

• Does the employee understand how improvement should be brought about?

• Is the employee motivated to improve?

• Does the employee know what will happen if no improvement occurs?

• Are plans for on-the-job follow-up clear?

• Did the interview result in a stronger relationship between the employee and the supervisor?

The supervisor should record the essential points of the interview and note anything that could have been done differently to make the interview more effective. It should be remembered that the interview is part of a continuing process of communication between supervisor and employee. The next step is follow-up.

5. policies & procedures

Those responsible for college personnel administration are confronted by three challenges: First, they must develop sound personnel policies and procedures to guide and enhance the recruitment, selection, compensation, development, and retention of staff. Second, these policies and procedures must be consistent with and representative of institutional philosophy. Third, they must satisfy the many complex federal and state laws and regulations that affect the college personnel function. Colleges must be able to meet these challenges in order to sustain a successful personnel program.

An effective employee communications program is integral to a comprehensive personnel program, and a policy and procedures manual is central to a successful communications program. The spectrum of employee communications ranges from short, periodic memoranda to extensive newsletters issued on a regular basis.

Policy and Procedures Manual

A policy and procedures manual or an employee handbook is a standard vehicle for communicating institutional policies and procedures to employees. Although there is not a uniform format, style, or approach for such manuals, they all should include several major sections:

1. Welcome and introduction, which is usually a message from the chief executive officer of the institution.

2. Basic information about the college, including purpose, size, type, history, and other, similar topics.

3. Employment policies and procedures—a comprehensive account of general working conditions, policies, work rules, and procedures.

4. Employee benefits, which includes detailed information on benefits such as insurance, retirement, vacations, sick leave and other leaves, and discounts.

5. Employee services, including information about such items as facilities, check cashing, and parking.

The manual or handbook should serve as a basic tool for new employee orientation as well as a useful reference for continuing employees. Supervisors should be thoroughly familiar with the manual to insure consistent administration of college policies and procedures. (See Exhibit

5A.) Such a manual need not be an expensive undertaking. Production costs can be kept to a minimum by using campus duplication equipment.

Personnel policies and procedures tend to change frequently; thus, there should be established avenues to inform employees regularly about such changes. One means is through a "Personnel Information Bulletin." Employees readily identify information with the personnel function when the communication carries its own distinctive letterhead. (See Exhibit 5B). An effective employee communications program incorporates the following objectives: (1) to inform employees in advance of a policy or procedure change, (2) to give employees the facts, that is, to discourage unfounded rumors, (3) to inform employees *why* something has happened or is being done, (4) to communicate the bad news along with the good, and (5) to encourage response from employees.

Essential Policy and Procedure Statements

The number of personnel policies and procedures varies among institutions, based on the philosophy of each. However, in every college, some of these should be reduced to writing for the benefit of both supervisors and employees. The following examples typify statements that should be incorporated into any institution's personnel policies and procedures documents. These can easily be adapted to fit any institution.

Probationary Period

The probationary period, an extension of the selection process, is described in Chapter 1. A sample statement from an employee handbook on a probationary period follows: "In order to become a continuing full-time employee, you will be required to successfully complete a probationary period of three working months. During this period, your supervisor will observe your performance to determine if you have the required abilities and qualifications to attain continuing status. The probationary period also provides you the opportunity to determine how well you like your job and the college. Prior to the expiration of the probationary period, your supervisor will evaluate your work performance on the 'Employee Performance Appraisal' form and indicate whether or not you will be awarded continuing status."

Once an employee has received continuing status, dismissal or discharge usually depends on a finding of "just cause," which requires documented evidence of rule or regulation violations that would warrant disciplinary action. In addition, due process procedures must be taken into consideration.

Performance Period

Many colleges require that an employee who is moved to an entirely different job demonstrate satisfactory performance in the new job during a "performance period" of 30 to 45 days. Continuing employees who transfer or are promoted to different jobs serve a performance period. This practice affords the new supervisor an opportunity to "try" an employee in a job without compelling the supervisor to retain the new employee if performance is not satisfactory. A sample performance period statement follows:

"An employee who is transferred or promoted to a different job classification will be required to complete a performance period of 45 work days. During this period, your supervisor will observe your performance to determine if you have the required abilities and qualifications to attain continuing status in the job classification."

Colleges with sizable staffs will frequently permit an employee who does not successfully complete a performance period to return to a job in the classification from which he or she was transferred or promoted. Smaller colleges often lack the position vacancies to afford employees this type of security. In such a situation, a general policy could be adopted which commits the college to attempt to place the unsuccessful employee in another position in the college.

Where this kind of policy is not feasible, institutions should provide some other assistance for employees who are promoted and are not successful in their new jobs; otherwise employees will become reluctant to apply for promotions. Careful selection criteria and realistic performance periods can minimize instances of unsatisfactory performance by promoted employees and can enhance a policy of "promotion from within."

Employment of Relatives

Most colleges have policies that restrict the employment of relatives, but there is a trend to liberalize antinepotism policies. An employer can restrict the employment of relatives, in situations where one would be supervisor of the other, without violating equal opportunity and affirmative action regulations, provided the policy is administered in a nondiscriminatory manner. Following is an example of a standard statement that is consistent with equal opportunity and affirmative action regulations: "Persons related by family or marriage may be employed by the college, provided such individuals meet regular college employment standards. However, faculty or staff members shall not initiate, participate in, or exercise any influence over departmental or institutional decisions involving a direct benefit to a member related by family or marriage (such benefits include initial appointment, retention, promotion, tenure, salary, leave of absence, and grievance adjustment). In situations where a conflict of interest might occur under normal operating procedures, the responsibility for the decision will pass to the next higher administrative level. For purposes of this policy, persons related by family or marriage are defined as a spouse, parent, child, individual for whom a faculty or staff member has been assigned legal responsibility in a guardianship capacity, sibling, grandparent, grandchild, aunt, uncle, niece, nephew, and in-laws."

Rest Periods or Breaks

Rest periods at the work place are common, with one break usually granted in the first half of the work shift and another in the second. Some employees have a tendency to "stretch" a rest period of ten or fifteen minutes into twice the time. A policy statement cannot, in and of itself, reduce abuses of the rest period, but it can and should serve as the basis for supervisory enforcement. Following is a sample rest period policy statement:

"A rest period of 15 minutes is granted in the first half of the employee's work shift and another rest period is allowed in the second half of the work shift. Rest periods are limited to 15 minutes of absence from the job. These periods are intended to be preceded and followed by an extended work period; thus, they may not be used to cover late arrival to work or early departure, nor may they be regarded as cumulative if not taken. Rest periods are to be scheduled by the supervisor and may be standardized or staggered among employees. A rest period of 15 minutes will be permitted at not less than two-hour intervals for work occurring immediately prior to or immediately following the regular work shift."

Working Hours and Schedules

The concept of a workweek for pay purposes evolved as public policy in the federal Wage and Hour Law. The provisions of this law remain applicable to independent colleges. However, the U.S. Supreme Court exempted *public* colleges from provisions of the law, except for the Equal Pay Amendments. (A comprehensive explanation of the Wage and Hour Law is included in NACUBO's *Federal Regulations and the Employment Practices of Colleges and Universities.)*

The law requires every employer to define a workweek for its employees. The workweek must consist of seven consecutive 24-hour periods (168 hours) that need not coincide with the calendar week; the workweek may begin on any day and at any hour of the day. A typical workweek statement is as follows: "The workweek for staff employees begins at 12:01 a.m. Sunday and runs continuously until 12:00 midnight Saturday." The workweek becomes the prime determinant for calculating overtime. Many public colleges, although exempt from the Wage and Hour Law, follow its overtime provisions because to do otherwise would probably be interpreted as denial of a benefit that is expected by their employees.

Overtime Pay

It is extremely important for colleges to define the conditions under which overtime pay and time off will be computed. *The Wage and Hour Law only requires payment at the rate of time and one-half the regular rate of pay for hours worked in excess of 40 hours in a workweek. It does not require overtime pay for hours worked in excess of 8 hours in a workday or for hours worked on a recognized holiday.* Frequently, however, prevailing practice or institutional policy requires such payment. A sample overtime policy statement follows:

"The statements in this policy are intended only to provide a basis for calculating straight time, overtime, and premium payments, and should not be construed as a guarantee of hours of work per day or per week. A workday is defined as a period of 24 consecutive hours, commencing with the beginning of the employee's regularly scheduled work shift. Overtime or premium pay at the rate of one and one-half the regular hourly rate will be paid for hours worked as follows:

A. All hours worked in excess of eight hours in any workday.

B. All hours worked in excess of forty hours in any workweek, provided that no pyramiding of overtime shall be applicable, that is, no employee shall be paid both daily and weekly overtime for the same hours worked.

C. All hours worked on a recognized college holiday.

D. Any recognized holiday for which the employee receives pay for not working will be counted as a day worked for computing weekly overtime."

Wage and Salary Policies and Procedures

Employees naturally have an interest in the wage and salary policies and procedures of the institution. Colleges should provide information to employees covering the schedule of paydays, frequency of wage adjustments, compensation formulas for promotions, salary ranges for jobs, work recall compensation arrangements, and shift premiums, if applicable. Wage and salary policies and procedures are described in Chapter 2, except for work recall and shift premium provisions, which are treated below.

Work Recall. Many employers provide additional remuneration or a guarantee of a minimum number of hours of compensation if an employee is called back to work outside scheduled work hours. This additional remuneration or guarantee of hours compensates the employee for inconvenience. A sample "work recall" statement follows:

"If an employee is called back to work outside his or her scheduled hours, necessitating an additional trip to and from work outside his or her normal workday, the employee will be paid a minimum of three hours for any service rendered of less than three hours on-the-job time. Overtime will be paid if such recall hours qualify under the overtime pay provisions."

Some work recall policies automatically compensate work recall hours at the overtime rate. The premium rate usually insures the availability of necessary personnel.

Shift Premiums. These generally serve to compensate inconvenience and to efficiently staff undesirable shifts. A sample shift premium statement follows:

"A shift premium will be accorded employees who are *regularly* assigned to the second and third shift as follows:

Second Shift: $.10 cents per hour. Second shift is any regularly scheduled shift starting between 2:00 p.m. and 10:00 p.m.

Third Shift: $.20 cents per hour. Third shift is any regularly scheduled shift starting between 10:00 p.m. and 5:00 a.m.

The shift premium is not applicable where the assignment occasionally varies or for temporary assignments of less than 30 days' duration."

Layoffs and Recalls

An equitable policy and procedure for layoffs is essential to a comprehensive personnel program. Most colleges experience some layoff of employees between academic terms or during the summer months. A sample layoff policy follows:

"One of the continuing benefits of employment with this college has been the stability of our employment patterns, which have shown a steady but controlled increase in the number of jobs. This has insured full-time, continuing employment for the majority of our employees. We have historically been able to predict the necessity for partial or temporary layoffs between academic terms or during the summer months. If it becomes necessary to reduce the work force, the following procedure will be followed:

A. Probationary and temporary employees will be laid off first, provided the employees retained can perform the available work.

B. Continuing employees will be laid off by job classification in reverse order of their length of service within the department or area in which they are employed, provided the employees with greater length of service possess the abilities and qualifications to perform the available work."

It is also common to state procedures for recalling employees from layoff, as in this sample statement: "Recall of employees from layoff will be in reverse order of their layoff. That is, the employee with the greatest amount of service who was laid off last will be recalled first, provided the employee is qualified to perform available work."

Grievance Procedure

Every employer should accord employees an organized method for adjusting grievances. Nonunion employers are frequently reluctant to do this, usually out of fear that they may relinquish management authority. However, one safeguard for retaining nonunion status is to accord employees a fair, impartial method for presenting and adjusting grievances.

Grievance procedures should provide for timely reviews and for adjustment of grievances at the lowest possible level. Usually, a fair and workable procedure can be developed with as few as two or three levels of review. Such procedures can provide for final resolution of a grievance within the college or for an advisory review by an outside third party. A sample grievance procedure follows:

"We recognize that problems involving employer-employee relations will arise from time to time. We believe that it is in the best interest of both the college and the employee to resolve these matters as soon as possible at the lowest possible level. In order that employees may be assured fair consideration of their problem(s), a means of review and appeal, without prejudice, to higher levels of authority has been established. Employee problems or concerns regarding college rules, regulations, working conditions, or their application should be taken up in the following manner:

"The employee should first attempt to adjust the grievance informally by discussing it with his or her immediate supervisor. If the matter is not adjusted to the employee's satisfaction through informal discussion, the employee may proceed to the formal grievance stage by presenting the grievance in writing to the immediate supervisor, describing the adjustment desired. The grievance must be presented to the immediate supervisor within 45 days of its occurrence. The supervisor will have five calendar days in which to provide the employee an answer in writing.

"If the employee is not satisfied with the answer from the immediate supervisor, he or she may take the grievance to the second level of review. The grievance must be presented in writing to the second level of review within five days from the time the answer was given or due by the immediate supervisor. The second level of review will be the next immediate level of authority, that is, the immediate supervisor's superior. The second-level reviewing officer will have five calendar days in which to provide the employee an answer in writing.

"If the employee is not satisfied with the answer received from the second level of review, he or she may take the grievance to the third and final level of review. The grievance must be presented to the third level of review within five days from the time the answer was given or due by the second-level reviewing officer. The third level of review will be the vice president of the respective area. The vice president will have ten calendar days in which to provide the employee an answer in writing. The decision of the vice president will be final and binding on all parties."

The number of levels of review and the reviewing officers must be determined by each institution. (See Exhibit 5C). Such a policy provides an internal, administrative remedy; it does not, of course, preclude outside action in the courts.

Rules, Regulations, and Disciplinary Action

Should the institution publish rules governing employee conduct? The correct answer may be either yes or no. An overwhelming majority of employers that are unionized have rules and regulations that are in writing. This is not because unionized employees need more guidance, but because of a basic labor relations principle: A union contract will normally include a grievance procedure that provides for binding arbitration for disputes arising between the parties. All matters related to disciplinary action are subject to the grievance procedure and, consequently, to eventual arbitration. One of the first considerations of an arbitrator in a disciplinary case is to determine if the employee had knowledge of the rules he or she is alleged to have violated. Management's best evidence to persuade the arbitrator of the employee's knowledge of rules is to demonstrate that they were issued in writing.

Nonunion employers frequently choose not to publish an extensive list of rules and regulations because they do not want to appear overly authoritarian or punitive to their employees. However, if an employee can be disciplined for violation of a rule, that employee can reasonably expect to be apprised of the rule through written communication. This is an area where the choice must be made individually by institution. (See Exhibits $5D_1$ and $5D_2$).

Progressive Discipline. Disciplinary action should be imposed only when absolutely necessary. Each incident that might require disciplinary action should be examined carefully to insure verification of the facts and consistent application of any disciplinary measures.

A useful approach to disciplinary action is that of "progressive discipline." This principle entails imposing increasingly severe forms of disciplinary action for repetition of an offense. For example, in a case where an employee is absent an excessive number of times, the supervisor might first warn the employee orally. If the pattern continues, the employee would receive a written warning. If the pattern still persists, the employee would be given a disciplinary suspension without pay for three days. If the abuse is not corrected, the employee might be given an additional suspension without pay for ten days. Finally, if there still is no improvement, the employee would be discharged. Progressive discipline may include fewer or more steps than this example. (See Exhibits $5E_1$, $5E_2$, and $5E_3$).

The principle of progressive discipline evolved from the labor relations environment. Arbitrators, in addition to considering whether or not an employee was aware of the rules, also consider whether or not an employee had advance knowledge of penalties that would result from violations.

Progressive discipline is not applicable in every instance where disciplinary action is warranted. The violation of some rules is so extreme that outright discharge is the only reasonable remedy. These violations would include, but not necessarily be limited to, theft, intoxication, willful destruction of college property, and unauthorized possession of firearms on campus.

Personnel Records and Information

Federal and state laws require the collection and retention of detailed personnel information. The specific data required and the retention schedules are generally included within the laws and supplementary explanatory bulletins.

Personnel records should be maintained for information that (1) is employment-related, (2) relates to wages and salaries, including benefits, (3) concerns disciplinary action, and (4) provides general personnel data. Most employers maintain separate file folders, or "employee personnel folders," for each employee. The information thus maintained varies among employees, but generally includes a chronological file of forms, letters, performance appraisals, etc., pertaining to the employee.

There is a growing trend in personnel administration to permit employees to have access to their personnel folders; it is likely that federal legislation will be enacted, comparable to the Family Educational Rights and Privacy Act of 1974—which affects students—that would make such access mandatory. Colleges should thus include only *relevant information* in personnel files. Since much of the personnel information maintained by employers is also applicable for payroll processing, colleges should be aware of potential costly duplication of records. Although payroll is primarily an accounting function, payroll and personel information should be coordinated for cost-effective management.

Small college administrators traditionally have not separated the personnel function from the payroll function. However, internal control is considered to be better if the two functions are separate, whereby personnel is the authorizing agent and payroll the processing agent. The paperwork required for authorization can be combined with other elements in the "change of status" form. The "change" form is a comprehensive document that includes information for all status-rate changes. (See Exhibits 1M₁ and 1M₂.)

Manual vs. Computerized Information

Information on payroll and personnel lends itself well to computerization, since these functions possess many common "data elements" that permit the design or purchase of comprehensive software packages for both at minimal cost. Many retail software packages for payroll and personnel provide "report generator" capabilities, including that of producing various management information reports (for example, payroll and personnel reports) while omitting the traditional computer programming routine. Many employers are also using "computer output microfilm" (microfilm or microfiche) as an inexpensive means of maintaining and retrieving personnel and payroll information.

Because many institutions maintain computer facilities on campus, the conversion of payroll and personnel information from the manual to the computerized mode can be accomplished at reasonable cost. Some employers have purchased minicomputers in order to process payroll and personnel records.

Collective Bargaining

Employees in higher education are unionizing at an increasing rate, which suggests that this trend may affect any institution, regardless of size, type, or location. Since 1970, independent colleges and universities with gross annual revenues in excess of $1,000,000 have been subject to the jurisdiction of the National Labor Relations Board (NLRB). This board is responsible for the administration and interpretation of national labor policy as stated in the Labor Management Relations Act (Taft-Hartley Act). The NLRB has the responsibility to promulgate procedures under which union representation elections may be conducted. While public colleges and universities are exempt from the jurisdiction of the NLRB, many states have enacted laws that accord state employees, including college employees, the right to bargain collectively.

In most instances in which a union is the exclusive bargaining agent, it bargains with the employer on all matters relating to wages, hours, and other terms and conditions of employment. In other words, almost anything is a potential subject for the bargaining process.

What to Expect if Unionization Occurs

Collective bargaining does not mean that productive work will grind to a halt, but it does bring with it a definite reduction of management's authority. Management's capacity to govern unilaterally will probably be impaired and flexibility in assigning, transferring, and promoting employees probably will be restricted. The institution's cost for supervisory staff and paperwork is likely to increase. Additional payroll time and costs will be incurred because of union dues checkoffs. Care must be taken that personnel records include documentation of incidents that result in disciplinary action. The institution will have to share some of its managerial decision making with the union and to bargain with the union on changes of shifts and working schedules, assignment of work, transfers and promotions, layoff procedures, and wages and benefits.

The college may become engaged in arbitration cases, each of which can cost many hours of supervisory time, attorneys' fees, and arbitrators' fees. The institution's right to discipline employees may be seriously impaired and it may occasionally be required to reinstate a discharged employee with back pay because of an arbitrator's decision. The college may lose its unrestricted right to use the most qualified employee on a specific job as well as the right to assign or require employees to work overtime. Many of the items mentioned above are typical content issues in union contracts.

An evaluation should be made of institutional conditions that could lead to unionization. What does a union organizer look for when planning an organizational drive? Some considerations are obvious: low wages, wage inequities, noncompetitive fringe benefits, arbitrary layoffs, arbitrary disciplinary action, shaky job security, and nonexistence of grievance procedures. Many colleges are vulnerable in these areas. A sound personnel program can correct these problems and assist a college to remain union-free.

Why Employees Join Unions

Following are the most common reasons why employees join unions:

1. *Lack of job security.* This appears to be a prime motivator for unionization; it includes failure to recognize seniority, arbitrary layoff, insufficient warnings before discharge, lack of grievance procedures, and arbitrary assignment and transfer practices.

2. *Noncompetitive wages and benefits.* This ranks high on the list. Unions generally have knowledge of competitive compensation packages offered by other employers and they may promise college employees that unionization can provide the same for them. Failure by the college to supply employees information on classification levels, salary ranges, and general wage information also fall into this category. The most damaging feature of all is wage favoritism, that is, different employees receiving different wages for comparable work. Unions will usually criticize any pay plan that provides different rates based on employee performance.

3. *Failure to advise employees what is expected of them.* This includes inconsistent performance appraisals by supervisors; unfair or inconsistent performance standards; and lack of uniformity in rules, regulations, and job assignments.

4. *Poor working conditions.* Lack of air conditioning, inadequate or expensive parking, and inadequate training and supervision are included in this category.

5. *Poor personnel policies and inconsistent administration of policies and procedures.* This includes failure to communicate policies or to state them in writing.

6. *Lack of advancement opportunities or favoritism in promotions.* Most employees wish to progress. They want to be rewarded for performance and for demonstrated abilities; lack of opportunity to do this may be a strong motivator toward unionization.

7. *Failure to consult employees on matters affecting their jobs.* This includes ignoring or discouraging suggestions from employees. If management doesn't listen, a union organizer will.

8. *Failure to keep employees informed.* Lack of communication has been the catalyst for many cases of unionization.

A major reason employees join unions is because of a need to "belong" and because each person must feel important as an individual. If a college fails to provide an environment that recognizes these basic human needs, its employees will seek other sources of satisfaction. Employees perceive that unions will provide them recognition, opportunity for participation, and a feeling of security. It has been said that unions don't *make* trouble; they *find* it.

The field of labor relations is extremely complex; dealing with it requires the expertise of a competent labor attorney, labor relations consultant, or personnel professional. At the first indication of labor discord, colleges should secure the services of a qualified labor relations professional if such expertise does not exist in the institution. Sound labor relations practices can reduce the severity of confrontation between an institution and unions.

Employees join unions because they perceive that unions will help to satisfy their needs; such needs are basic to human aspirations and endeavors, regardless of whether or not a union is involved. An effective personnel program, which is concerned with the needs of employees, is a key requirement for harmonious employee relations and for good college management.

Exhibit 5A

How To Set Up a Policy and Procedures Manual

The following article was prepared by Bettye H. Galloway, of the University of Mississippi, for the "How-to" series published by the College and University Personnel Association.

The primary purpose of a policy and procedures manual is to present an institution's policies, to describe in detail the rules and regulations governing an institution, and to indicate procedures for implementing these. The manual should cover policies and procedures adopted by the institution, edicts issued by the governing board, and applicable federal and state laws.

A policy manual generally differs from a handbook in that the latter is usually smaller and summarizes policies, whereas a manual describes them completely. For example, where a handbook would indicate that official travel is reimbursable, a manual would not only define "official travel," but would include the entire travel policy, together with instructions and examples on when and how to request travel, to have the trip approved, to receive a cash advance, and to file the reimbursement voucher.

A manual should be organized with the policy statement first, followed by the procedures for implementing the policy; in many cases, the forms used in implementation are included for clarification. When policies and procedures are combined in one volume, cross-references are easily effected, and chances of error are reduced.

A policy manual serves as a central source for official reference and it should be printed in a loosclcaf form to accommodate periodic supplementation. Procedures may change more often than the policies themselves and they should also be kept up-to-date.

Responsibility for the Manual

An institution's central personnel office is most often the recipient of inquiries concerning rules and regulations governing an institution and thus should be assigned the responsibility for preparing and maintaining a policy manual. Most of the functions of the personnel office come under the auspices of adopted policy; therefore, this office is intimately acquainted with administration of the policies and is more likely to be aware of any changes or additions.

Securing the Information

A collection should be made of all the rules and regulations that govern the employees and the operation of the institution. This information should be grouped into logical sections for compiling the manual. When exact copies of official regulations have been obtained, intensive research should be conducted to determine exactly how the policy is properly implemented. Copies of forms should be secured, and a step-by-step procedure for implementing the policy should be outlined. Preparing the material for the manual involves stating the official policy, presenting completed samples of the forms used for implementing the policy, advising where to secure the forms, and presenting instructions for routing and follow-up procedures.

Organizing the Information

Policy manual sections should include groupings such as "Employment Policies," "Benefits," and "General Policies." These should be harmonious with the subdivisions and general operations of the institution; if policies differ from department to department or from campus to campus, specific information should be given as to their application in each unit. A *sample grouping* follows:

Employment Policies
Annual leave
  Vacation
  Sick Leave
  Maternity Leave
  Leave Without Pay
Classification Plan
Demotions
Employment of Relatives
Equal Opportunity
Faculty Salary Levels
Grievances
Hours of Work
Layoffs
Preemployment Physical
  Examinations
Postdoctoral Research Associates
Recruitment
Separation from Employment
Tenure
Transfers

Benefits
Business Pursuits Liability Insurance
Disability Income Protection
Further Education

Group Life Insurance
Health and Hospitalization
  Insurance
Scholarships for Children of Faculty
  and Staff
Social Security
Tax-Sheltered Annuities
Worker's Compensation

General Policies
Academic Regulations
Campus Speakers
Cash Receipts and Reports
Commencement
Committees
Faculty Meetings
Fair Labor Standards Act
Housing
Research Grants and Contracts
Traffic Regulations
Travel

The table of contents should list items in sequential order, and an index should be devised for quick reference, with a view to the differences in terminology among employees. For instance, "vacation" should be indexed as well as "annual leave," and "minimum wage" and "pay rates" should be listed in addition to "salary scales."

Distributing Changes in the Manual

A systematic procedure should be adopted for reviewing and supplementing the manual. Six-month intervals usually suffice, and December and July are usually excellent months for issuing supplements—December for issuing changes occurring effective with the new calendar year and July for the beginning of the new fiscal year. However, policy changes requiring immediate action should be circulated as soon as they occur. One manual should be set up as a control volume and changes should be noted as they occur by a person assigned this responsibility. At the end of November or June, these changes should be organized, written, and printed for distribution.

Each page of the supplement should be dated and the page numbered. Should the replacement section be longer than the existing section, the numbering should run to subsections, for example, pages 24, 25, 25a, and 25b.

A memorandum should accompany each mailing with appropriate instructions, such as: "Delete page 22, dated March 1979, and insert page 22, dated July 1980; Delete pages 28 and 29, dated July 1979, and insert pages 28, 29, 29a, and 29b, dated July 1980." In addition to providing instructions for insertion, this memorandum serves as a transmittal record and allows each person responsible for maintaining the manual to make sure that all of the new pages have been received.

At the time of initial publication and distribution, a list of names should be compiled of those persons who receive a manual; usually, these are department heads. Supplements are addressed to individuals rather than to offices; in this way one person is responsible for the maintenance of the manual in each office.

Supplements should be issued in the same format as the manual, that is, the policy statement should appear first, followed by the procedures.

Exhibit 5B

CSUN PERSONNEL INFORMATION BULLETIN

EMPLOYEES' TIME OFF TO VOTE

The California State Election Code, Section 14350, provides for the following:

"If a voter does not have sufficient time outside of working hours to vote at a statewide election, the voter may, without loss of pay, take off enough working time which when added to the voting time available outside of working hours will enable the voter to vote.

"No more than two hours of the time taken off for voting shall be without loss of pay. The time off for voting shall be only at the beginning or end of the regular working shift, whichever allows the most free time for voting and the least time off from the regular working shift, unless otherwise mutually agreed.

"If the employee on the third working day prior to the day of election, knows or has reason to believe that time off will be necessary to be able to vote on election day, the employee shall give the employer at least two working days' notice that time off for voting is desired, in accordance with the provisions of this section."

The above section requires that employees be given paid time off to vote only if the employee does not have sufficient time to vote outside of working hours. Since the polls are normally open from 7:00 a.m. to 8:00 p.m., in most cases employees of this university will be able to vote outside of working hours and, thus, should not be given time off. It is only in special cases, such as when an employee is required to work overtime, the polls are open only for a limited time, or some other equally good reason, that employees would need to be given paid time off to vote. However, when a good reason does exist, an employee is entitled by law to be paid time off to vote.

If you have any questions, please contact the Personnel Office.

Exhibit 5C

STAFF COMPLAINT PROCEDURE

It is the purpose of the Staff Complaint Procedure to establish a method whereby complaints of staff members will be resolved promptly. The filing of a complaint will in no way prejudice the service or status of the staff member. Please see the _____ Faculty and Staff Manual for a full description of this procedure.

Staff Member _____ Date _____

Department _____ Job Title _____ Employment Date _____

Statement of Complaint; Background/activity leading to complaint, including dates:

_____

_____

_____

Remedy Requested: _____

Staff Member's Signature _____ Date _____

1 Decision _____ Hearing Date _____

_____

_____

Complaint Resolved   Yes ☐   No ☐   Staff Member _____ Date _____

Request Appeal   Yes ☐   No ☐   Supervisor _____ Date _____

2 Decision _____ Hearing Date _____

_____

_____

Complaint Resolved   Yes ☐   No ☐   Staff Member _____ Date _____

Request Appeal   Yes ☐   No ☐   Supervisor _____ Date _____

3 Decision _____ Hearing Date _____

_____

_____

Complaint Resolved   Yes ☐   No ☐   Staff Member _____ Date _____

Request Appeal   Yes ☐   No ☐   Director Institutional Services _____ Date _____

4 (FINAL) Decision _____ Hearing Date _____

_____

_____

_____

Vice Chancellor: _____ Date _____

Exhibit 5D$_1$

(This example is from a unionized *institution)*

Rules, Regulations, and Discipline Procedures

In order to maintain and operate the college in the best interest of all concerned, it is necessary that all employees adhere to certain standards of conduct. Employees who violate these rules and regulations will be subject to disciplinary action that includes (but is not limited to) the following:

1 Verbal Warning   3 Three-Day Suspension
2 Written Warning   4 Up to and Including Discharge

These penalties may vary, *at the sole discretion of the college*, where there are extenuating circumstances, including prior unlike violations.

Examples of violations and the probable penalties for such violations are set forth as follows:

EXAMPLES OF VIOLATIONS

Offense	Step I	Step II	Step III	Step IV
1. Excessive tardiness.	1	2	3	4
2. Excessive absenteeism.	1	2	3	4
3. Careless or substandard workmanship resulting in waste, spoilage or delay.	1	2	3	4
4. Posting, defacing, or removing notices from college bulletin boards or other public places.	1	2	3	4
5. Failure to report for accepted overtime work without a justifiable reason, or failure to promptly notify the college of such absence.	1	2	3	4
6. Engaging in horseplay or scuffling.	1	2	3	4
7. Leaving the work location during work shift without authorization.	1	2	3	4
8. Idling, loafing, or inattention during work hours.	1	2	3	4
9. Failure to properly ring time clock.	1	2	3	4
10. Failure to notify supervisor on each day of unscheduled absence.	1	2	3	4
11. Using profane or obscene language or gestures.	1	2	3	4

Offense	Step I	Step II	Step III	Step IV
12. Violations of minor safety rules and practices.	1	2	3	4
13. Misusing, damaging, or destroying college property.	2	3	4	
14. Gambling or possession of gambling devices on college property.	2	3	4	
15. Insubordination.	3	4		
16. Violations of major safety rules and practices.	3	4		
17. Sleeping or giving the impression of sleeping during work hours.	3	4		
18. Ringing another employee's time card.	3	4		
19. Falsifying or altering time cards or other records.	3	4		
20. Reporting to work while under the influence of alcoholic beverages or narcotics, or possession or use of these on college property.	3	4		
21. Immoral conduct or indecency.	3	4		
22. Fighting, assault, attempted assault, or threatening anyone on college property.	4			
23. Unexcused absence of three consecutive days.	4			
24. Conviction in a civil or criminal court or detention by law enforcement authorities without a reason acceptable to the college.	4			
25. Theft of employee or college property.	4			
26. Unauthorized possession of weapons or explosives on college property.	4			
27. Any other conduct which is inconsistent with proper behavior.	Penalty to be assessed on circumstances.			
28. Multiple violations, whether or not simultaneous, of the foregoing rules and regulations.	Penalty to be assessed on circumstances.			
29. Falsification of employment application.	Penalty to be assessed on circumstances.			

Exhibit 5D₂   (This example is from a nonunion institution)

Discipline Procedures for Buildings and Grounds Employees

Employees will be subject to disciplinary action for any of the following offenses:

1. Theft of college property. First offense, discharge.
2. Unreported absence of three or more days. First offense, discharge.
3. Immoral conduct or indecency. First offense, discharge.
4. Falsifying employment application. First offense, discharge.
5. Drinking alcoholic beverages during work hours, or on campus at any time. First offense, discharge.
6. Insubordination. First offense, one week suspension without pay; second offense, discharge.
7. Reporting to work under the influence of alcohol or drugs. First offense, one week suspension without pay; second offense, discharge.
8. Falsifying time cards or work records. First offense, written warning; second offense, discharge.
9. Punching out a time card for someone else. First offense, written warning; second offense, discharge.
10. Sleeping on job during work hours. First offense, one week suspension without pay; second offense, discharge.
11. Fighting or horseplay. First offense, verbal warning; second offense, written warning; third offense, one week suspension without pay.
12. Excessive absenteeism or tardiness. First offense, verbal warning; continuation, written warning; further continuation, discharge.
13. Violating a safety rule or practice. First offense, verbal warning; second offense, written warning; third offense, one week suspension without pay.

Other offenses that violate standards of honesty and ethical relationships—which are especially necessary in a college community—will also be subject to disciplinary action.

The following policy is applicable if an employee in this department feels that a disciplinary action has been unfair:

1. First, the employee must discuss the reasons for discipline with the superintendent of buildings and grounds. This discussion must take place within three days after the disciplinary action.
2. If still not satisfied, the employee may appeal the decision to the vice president for business, who shall conduct a hearing. Any party shall be entitled to present witnesses or documents in support of his or her position. The decision of the vice president for business shall be final, but he or she shall consult with the president of the college in appeals from discharge decisions.

Exhibit 5E₁

DEPARTMENT OF PHYSICAL PLANT

Verbal Warning Form

_____

Date of Warning

I have today given verbal warning to employee(s) _____

_____

_____

Classification _____

Persons present _____

_____

Reasons for warning: _____

_____

_____

_____

_____

_____

_____

_____

_____

(Use other side if necessary)

Date and hour of violation_____ _____

                                 (Date)   (Hour)

_____

Supervisor's Signature

Exhibit 5E₂

Notice of Written Warning

_____
Date

TO: _____   _____
         Employee's Name   Title

Reason for Warning

You have been issued this *written warning* for violation of a college rule or regulation which reads as follows:

_____

_____

_____

The violation occurred on (date) _____ at
(time) _____ at the following location _____.

Facts Related to Violation (Be Specific Regarding Circumstances Involved)

_____
_____
_____
_____
_____

Please note that your file contains previous warnings for violation of college rules or regulations as follows:

_____ _____/_____ _____/_____ _____
Date Type of Warning Date Type of Warning Date Type of Warning

Future violations of college rules or regulations will result in disciplinary suspension or discharge.

Distribution: _____
  Original—Employee   Supervisor's Signature
  1 Copy —Personnel Services   _____
  1 Copy —Department   Title

Exhibit 5E₃

Notice of Disciplinary Suspension

_____
Date

TO: _____   _____
     Employee's Name   Title

Disciplinary Suspension

You are hereby suspended without pay for _____ workdays effective

_____ _____ until _____ _____.
   Date   Time   Date   Time

Reason for Suspension

You have been issued this disciplinary suspension for violation of a college rule or regulation which reads as follows:

_____

_____

_____.

The violation occurred on (date) _____ at (time) _____ at the following location _____.

Facts Related to Violation (Be Specific Regarding Circumstances Involved)

_____

_____

_____

_____

Future violations of college rules or regulations will result in further disciplinary suspension or discharge.

Distribution·
  Original—Employee
  1 Copy —Personnel Services
  1 Copy —Department

_____
Supervisor's Signature

_____
Title

glossary

Central tendency In performance appraisal, a tendency to rate all employees within a narrow range, usually toward the middle (page 130).

Change of status form A form used to record and implement changes in an employee's work status, such as changes in salary, position, leave status, and others (page 16).

Class A group of positions that are similar in their responsibilities and in duties performed, require essentially the same education and experience, and can equitably be placed in the same pay grade and rate range (page 70).

Class specification A description of the typical responsibilities, duties, and qualification requirements of a class (page 90).

Demotion Movement to a position in a lower pay grade (page 166).

Employment requisition A form used by a department to communicate to the centralized employment office the desire to fill a vacant position (page 5).

Exempt A term used to describe jobs that are exempt from the overtime pay requirements of the Fair Labor Standards Act (page 65).

Halo effect In performance appraisal, a tendency to rate all traits or factors as equal to one trait or factor because the rater was favorably or unfavorably impressed by performance concerning the one factor (page 130).

Job An assignment of work that has responsibilities, duties, and tasks different from other work assignments (page 65).

Job analysis The process of collecting and analyzing information concerning the responsibilities, duties, organizational relationships, and educational and experiential requirements of jobs (page 65).

Job classification The process of assigning jobs to pay grades through the use of job evaluation (page 5).

Job description A listing of the responsibilities and duties assigned to a job and the qualifications to perform same (pages 5,66).

Job evaluation A systematic method of determining the fair value or difficulty of a particular job in relation to all other jobs (page 67).

Job relatedness test A result of the Griggs v. Duke Power Company case, which requires that any qualification used as a condition of employment must bear a significant relation to successful job performance (page 6).

Job specification   A specialized job description, often emphasizing personal qualifications, which is used to facilitate recruitment and selection (page 5).

Leniency tendency   In performance appraisal, a tendency to rate all employees high on all factors (page 130).

Needs assessment   In the personnel context, the identification of training and development needs (page 123).

Nonexempt   A term used to describe jobs that are *not* exempt from the overtime pay requirements of the Fair Labor Standards Act (page 65).

Performance period   A working test period commencing with the promotion of an employee to a new job and usually terminating 30 to 60 days later (pages 17,154).

Position   A group of responsibilities and of duties to be performed by one employee. When several persons are doing similar work, each has the same job but a different position (page 5).

Position control system   A manual or computer system designed to identify and record personnel history for each budgeted position (page 4).

Position description   A listing of the responsibilities and duties assigned to a position and the qualifications required to perform same (pages 5,66).

Probationary period   A working test period commencing immediately on employment and usually terminating 60 to 90 days later (pages 16,153).

Progressive discipline   The administration of increasingly more severe forms of disciplinary action based on repetition of an offense (page 160).

Promotion   Movement to a position in a higher pay grade (page 17).

Recency error   In performance appraisal, a tendency to base a rating on that which is most easily remembered- usually the employee's most recent behavior (page 130).

Red circle rates   A term used to describe a wage rate or salary that falls below the minimum or above the maximum of a wage-salary range (page 78).

Salary   A term generally used to describe a monthly rate of pay (page 63).

Salary grade (wage grade)   A grouping of jobs of comparable responsibility or difficulty, as determined by job evaluation (page 76).

Severity tendency   In performance appraisal, a tendency to be overly critical of performance because of unrealistic or unachievable performance standards (page 130).

Shift premium (differential)   Additional compensation paid to employees who work night shifts (page 157).

Transfer   Movement to a position in the same pay grade (page 17).

Turnover rate   A measurement referring to the number of employees separated from the payroll during a stated period (page 20).

Underrepresentation   In applicant pools, lacking a sufficient number of females and minorities as compared to the availability of these groups in appropriate labor recruiting markets (page 8–15).

Underutilization   In a workforce, lacking a sufficient number of females and minorities as compared to the availability of these groups in appropriate labor recruiting markets (page 8–15).

Wage   A term generally used to describe an *hourly* rate of pay (page 63).

Work recall (call back pay)   Guaranteed compensation, usually at a premium rate, for employees who are called to work outside of their normal shifts (page 157).

Workweek   A continuous period of 168 hours (7 days of 24 hours each) used primarily as a basis for calculating overtime pay as required by the Fair Labor Standards Act (page 155).

bibliography

Belcher, David W. *Wage and Salary Administration*. Englewood Cliffs, NJ: Prentice Hall, 1962.

Brennan, Charles W. *Wage Administration*. Homewood, IL: Richard D. Irwin, Inc., 1966.

College and University Personnel Association. *Administrative Compensation Survey* (updated annually). Washington, DC: The Association.

_____. *Women and Minorities (1975–76)*, a supplement to the *Administrative Compensation Survey* (see above). Washington, DC: The Association.

_____. "How-to" Series. Rev. ed. Washington, DC: The Association, 1980.

_____. *Personnel Policy Models*. 2nd ed. Washington, DC: The Association, 1980.

Indiana State Chamber of Commerce. *Employer's Labor Relations Guidebook*. Indianapolis, IN: The Chamber, 1975.

Julius, Michael J. *Personnel Management*. Homewood, IL: Richard D. Irwin, Inc., 1963.

Lopez, Felix M. *Evaluating Employee Performance*. Chicago, IL: Public Personnel Association, 1968.

National Association of College and University Business Officers. The Administrative Service: 2:7, "Personnel"; 2:7:1. "A Personnel Data Base"; 2:7:2, "Employee Performance Appraisal"; 2:8, "Faculty and Staff Benefits"; and 2:9, "Labor Relations and Collective Bargaining." (A subscription service.) Washington, DC: The Association.

_____. *Federal Regulations and the Employment Practices of Colleges and Universities*. (A subscription service.) Washington, DC: The Association.

Public Personnel Association. *Employee Training and Development in the Public Service*. Chicago, IL: The Association, 1970.